GOOD
INTENTIONS
BAD
CONSEQUENCES
VOTERS' INFORMATION PROBLEMS

PHILLIP NELSON

Printed in the United States of America

Library of Congress Control Number: 2020907470
ISBN: Softcover   978-1-64908-151-3
         eBook   978-1-64908-150-6

Republished by: PageTurner Press and Media LLC
Publication Date: 06/12/2020

To order copies of this book, contact:

PageTurner Press and Media
Phone: 1-888-447-9651
order@pageturner.us
www.pageturner.us

TABLE OF CONTENTS

How these three fundamental voter concerns arose in the context of voters' incentive to imitate their associates. Naïve altruism is concern for others without taking into account the unintended consequences of any policy. I argue that this is the initial kind of altruism that is sustained by confirmation bias, preferring evidence that agrees with previous beliefs.

The emphasis is on the differences by fields in professor behavior. The claim is that those differences provide insight into the motivations governing professors' political preferences. Of particular importance is the difference between the political preferences of economists and the rest of the social sciences and the humanities. I defend the proposition that this difference is attributable to the naïve altruism of the latter. I then look at the impact of the college experience on its students, particularly lawyers, journalists, and teachers, both college and non-college.

Naïve altruists understate the monetary costs of the policies they prefer and prefer them less when informed of the true costs. Similarly, most Americans are in favor of higher minimum wages without examining the unintended consequences of that policy. When informed of those consequences their support of that policy is significantly reduced.

This chapter shows how some commonly observed characteristics of voting behavior in the United States can be explained by the processes on which this book focuses: the liberalism of urban areas, the increase in conservatism with age, and the conservatism associated with church attendance and how those associations can be reversed under special circumstances.

This chapter defends a somewhat different approach to value statements. It starts with a value tautology: for the purpose of giving people what they want we define "good" as what people would want if they had sufficient information. The important proposition in that chapter is that there would be less naïve altruists if they were informed about the unintended consequences of their policy preferences.

Even with sufficient information there will be individual differences in political preferences. There is general agreement that the democratic ideal would be the appropriate way to resolve those differences. Representative democracy with the rule of law is the best approximation we have to that ideal. We examine what that tells us about appropriate policy.

This chapter looks at two liberal ideas. First, that the rich have too much influence in determining government redistribution. It shows that the rich have less power in determining redistribution by income classes. Instead its power is focused on special interest returns.

Second, that concern with status creates a negative income externality, which helps to justify government redistribution and environmental policy. The chapter shows that there are many processes that produce a positive externality, in particular the increased trust produced by higher income and the increased risk taken by higher income groups. There are also features of the status market that produce positive income externalities.

CHAPTER 1

OVERVIEW

Political scientists have written extensively about voters' lack of information, but they have ignored one of the most important voter information problems: lack of information about the consequences of the policies they advocate. This problem is particularly severe among voters who want to "do good" but are uninformed about essential features of their attempts to do so. It is the information problems of that group of voters that generates the main distinction between what voters intend and the consequences these intentions produce.

The disagreement between liberals and conservatives about economic policy is focused on two questions. Should governments spend more directly and indirectly on protecting the environment? Should governments redistribute more income to the poor and away from the wealthy? Answers to these questions are of more than passing interest to social scientists and citizens alike.

In logic these answers require a comparison of 'what is' and 'what is better', and some feasible path to get toward the latter from the former. Better information is the path advocated in this book. It is feasible because it does not require voters to acquire more information than they have incentives to acquire, just better information, which need not be more expensive information.

For the most part, the economics literature has used a simple self-interest model to explain political choices, and certain features of political preferences are consistent with that model such as the direct relationship between income and votes for Republicans. But that is not the whole story, and this book focuses on the rest of the story. Both self-interest and altruism affect voter decisions. However, both of these motivations will be somewhat muted because they both focus on the policy consequences of voting. Any individual voter has a negligible effect on those consequences because his vote has a negligible impact on voting outcomes. In contrast, voters are primarily interested in others' reaction to their vote and how they view themselves, largely a function of others' potential reactions. As a result, self-interest does not play the dominant role in determining political decisions that it plays in determining market decisions. The political position of limousine liberals is the most obvious deviation from the income determinant of political choice by way of self-interest. Indeed, Nelson and Greene, 2003 found that self-interest variables were less important than other variables in determining political positions. But still self-interest plays a role in voter choice, just not the overwhelming role it plays in market decisions.

The reason self-interest and altruism affects voter decisions at all is that voter preferences are simply extensions of the preferences they express in conversation, and people do talk about their self-interested preferences and their notions of what is good for the world and their country. These latter notions of what is good are often influenced by self-interest, but not always.

That the individual voter has a negligible effect on voting outcomes has another important effect. Voters, for the most part, have little self-interested incentive to acquire much information about the consequences of government policy. To the extent they have any political information at all, it is a consumption good. The usual way of determining how much political information voters have is finding how many political facts they know. Even by this standard, many voters are ill informed. But there is an equally important political knowledge component—knowledge of the consequences of policies. As I try to show in this book, many voters are also ill informed with respect to this component. Many of the voters who know their political facts are woefully deficient in their knowledge of policy consequences, and this has profound effects on their voting behavior.

One such effect is a certain erratic nature of voting outcomes. There are multiple motivations in voting. The motivation that dominates voting at any one time can vary. Occasionally xenophobia dominates. Hitler's election, the Know Nothing party in the United States and the Know Nothing

Party are examples of this phenomenon. Their success is also attributable to a disgust with stalemates sometimes produced by representative democracy. But, for the most part other reasons for voting are at the fore.

The divide in the electorate on which I concentrate is between two groups. One group includes those who vote in a self-interested way, those who are traditionalists, and those who vote the same way as the first two because they imitate their vote. The other group is those voting altruistically in a particular way and those whose vote imitates the former. I call that way liberal altruism and I call the above bifurcation the "great divide".

Liberal altruistic voters advocate more government expenditures for the same causes for which most people give to charities with one notable exception – religious causes. Liberal altruistic voters advocate more government expenditures for the sick, the poor, the environment, education, etc., all charitable causes The rationale for calling this a form of altruism is that the objects of charity are determined by an altruistic process. Charities survive only if they respond to at least some people's view of some social need not satisfied by self-interested actions. The reason the charity for religious purposes is not included in liberal altruism is that liberals are relatively unreligious.

As detailed in this book, there is a good deal of evidence that there is an innate altruistic preference. But there are serious problems with liberal altruistic voting. Currently, people cannot observe directly many of the consequences of their actions and the list of liberal altruistic actions has grown considerably. Now people have to acquire their information indirectly about those consequences. That indirectness creates a serious bias, the well-known confirmation bias. People tend to look for information that confirms their current views and avoid contrary information. Liberal altruistic voters have no incentive to acquire information that would call into question their political preferences, sustained as they are by the political preferences of their liberal altruistic friends. In consequence, liberal altruistic voters tend to continue to be liberal altruistic voters in spite of a good deal of evidence that they ignore. The most important ignored consequences of their agenda are the unintended consequences of their actions. That is the justification for calling liberal altruistic voters naïve.

Confirmation bias is not the only reason naïve altruists do not examine unintended consequences. Many do not examine consequences at all. They focus simply on intentions. They support candidates who are empathetic, that is who have their hearts in the right place. But there is a significant difference between intentions and consequences. The justification for a free market is Adam Smith's invisible hand, that in a market economy self-interested decisions lead to socially desirable consequences. There are, indeed, all sorts of market imperfections that prevent a one-to-one correspondence between self-interest and the socially desirable. However, those imperfections are not so great that they prevent capitalism from producing favorable social results on average, favorable as participants evaluate those results. Those favorable results occur in spite of no such intentions from the market players. Those favorable results have to be compared with government alternatives which are at least somewhat motivated by good intentions but have serious unintended consequences.

Economists claim, with varying degrees of consensus, a whole range of unintended consequences of the naïve altruistic voting associated with liberals. There is the greater unemployment generated by the minimum wage, a reduction in the quantity and quality of products produced by price controls, a reduction in risk taking generated by taxing the rich, an increase in single mothers and a decrease in education produced by assorted indirect consequences of welfare programs. In the next chapter I detail those claims but I do not establish them. In that respect I depend on the work of others, though the unintended consequences listed are implications of simple economics.

These consequences tend to be unfavorable as evaluated both by the people being helped and by the liberal altruistic voter himself, using their own criteria of what constitutes "unfavorable". From the point of view of the liberal altruistic voter those unfavorable consequences need not be so great that they outweigh the direct benefits of his actions. But they are great enough to induce at least some altruistic voters to change their votes when they discover those unintended consequences. The book presents evidence that the unintended consequences of political decisions are often ignored. It also shows how information about those consequences can change voter preferences.

One does not have to go very far to see the impact of the unintended consequences of government actions. Costs are an unintended consequence of government expenditures and most regulations. But these costs are almost invariably ignored or understated by the advocates of these policies. Governments go to great length to hide the costs of their policies. Deficit financing is one such means. Though deficits postpone taxes, there is no postponing the use of resources that can be used otherwise, what the literature calls alternative costs. It is not accidental that those in favor of greater government spending are deficit advocates compared to those who are opposed to such spending. Indirect taxes and making business's pay are other actions that decrease the probability that voters are aware of costs or grossly underestimate them.

There is also evidence that voters who are aware of their personal costs caused by any particular government action are less in favor of that action. However, that evidence is scantier. The best evidence is the efforts of spending advocates to hide costs, though there can be other reasons for some of these efforts. For example, deficits make some sense during recessions but not through the whole business cycle.

I have excluded one group in our great divide—less naïve altruists. One objective of this book is to determine where they belong in the liberal-conservative spectrum. So that is a conclusion to be reached rather than a presupposition. We do look at the behavior of the less naïve voters, but outside the framework of the "great divide".

The divide between naive altruistic and non-altruistic voting can be somewhat confusing. Different people can vote for the same policy for altruistic or self-interested reasons. Those on welfare can vote for greater welfare payments while those neither on welfare or potentially on welfare can vote similarly for altruistic reasons. But the comparison for our purposes is between altruistic voting and self-interested voting in the aggregate. There are many self-interested who do not gain from an increase in welfare payments so that aggregate self-interested votes would be less in favor of increased welfare payments than the votes of naïve altruists.

Then again, some people will vote altruistically in certain contexts but not in others. Still this book provides evidence that the division is clear enough to generate significant differences in voting behavior. Probably, the clearest implication is the case of responses to local environmental problems. By definition, the self-interested consequences of these responses -- both the benefits and the costs-- are largely confined to a locality. Self-interested voting would, therefore, be confined to that locality. Others, who are at all concerned, would engage in altruistic voting, largely of the naïve sort. They would opt for a better environment without any consideration of costs.

An example of the voting implications of this phenomenon is the difference in local and non-local attitudes toward oil drilling in ANWAR, the Alaska National Wildlife Reserve. Alaskans are overwhelmingly in favor of that drilling even though it is they who experience any of the unfavorable environmental consequences of that drilling. Non locals are sufficiently opposed so that such drilling continues to be prohibited by the national government. Of course, drilling in ANWAR has consequences beyond Alaska. Most of those non local consequences are favorable to non-Alaskans, chiefly reduced oil prices. However, those relatively minor effects for the non-Alaskans are not enough to counter the returns from environmental advocacy, advocacy that occurs even though they barely experience the environmental impact of Alaskan oil drilling. It should be noted that this opposition occurred before concerns with climate change created opposition to fossil fuels in general. It was concern about the fate of caribou and the wilds in general that were the dominant foci of the opposition to oil drilling in ANWAR.

Many phenomenon that are otherwise unexplained make sense because of the great divide. University teachers, especially those in the humanities and the non-economic social sciences, are more liberal than others. One of the rationales for the existence of social scientists is to find ways to make society better. In fulfilling that job they are naive altruists for the most part. All that is required is advocating government actions favoring the same causes that charities have favored. In consequence, naïve altruism is the natural starting position of altruists. Because altruists start out as naïve altruists, confirmation bias tends to keep them in that state of naivety. Some universities have even institutionalized confirmation bias. They have created "safe spaces" where students can go to avoid ideas that make them uncomfortable, though most universities hardly need those spaces for students to avoid sparse uncomfortable ideas. The easiest way to practice confirmation bias is to avoid uncomfortable ideas which many in universities do by avoiding them with or without "safe spaces."

There is one group of social scientists who share an altruistic interest in policy with the others but who are not overwhelmingly naïve: economists. Many systematically examine the unintended consequences of government policy.

For example, a standard feature of elementary microeconomics is a demonstration of the reduced real income resulting from price controls. In consequence, their views on policy are dramatically more conservative than the rest of the social sciences. This is because the bulk of unintended consequences of the policies of naïve altruists are unfavorable, as demonstrated later in this book. However, economists play a relatively minor role in determining the overall effect of colleges in determining political positions, as witnessed by the overwhelmingly liberal character of universities.

Because of their important influence on many, including the media and lawyers, university teachers play an important role in determining political attitudes. Take the positive relationship between age and conservatism. Most people with altruistic tendencies start as naïve altruists. Their exposure to the educational system fortifies that naïve altruism. They then are influenced by their friends and associates. If their friends are all fellow naïve altruists, they continue in their naïve altruistic ways. The more non-naïve altruistic friends they have, the more they modify their voting away from naive altruism. The average of these effects must be toward self-interested voting and traditionalism because the educational influence is more than averagely toward naive altruistic voting. Ones' friends on average will be more conservative than the educators people have encountered. The longer the impact of socializing after education, the more conservative we would expect a person to be.

In a world where education is liberalizing in the political sense one would expect any process that increased socializing to make one more conservative. That explains why church attendance makes one more conservative in spite of church sermons which are often quite liberal. Church attendance is an important way to make and keep friends.

But socializing changes political positions only if that socializing involves people whose political positions are different from one's own. People, however, prefer to socialize with people with similar political views. The denser the population, the easier it is to make that preference a reality. In consequence, the conservative impact of socializing would be smaller for big cities.

All these predictions are turned on their head when universities are opposed to more government intervention in the economy. Such a situation occurred in Eastern Europe after the Cold War. The past was a past of massive government intervention in the economy. The importation of ideas from the West made intellectuals oppose such behavior. Then, the aged and the countryside would be relative proponents of that past of massive government expenditures.

Through the internet, there has been a vast increase in the sources of political information available to voters. Paradoxically, however, this increase in the sources available, reduces the range of information acquired by voters. Confirmation bias is at work. Voters prefer information sources that confirm their political positions. With more sources of information it is easier for voters to put that preference to work. The result is more voter partisanship. I suspect this is the reason for the increase in partisanship in the Western world frequently noted by observers. Through this specialization of voters, internet sources have an incentive to become more specialized themselves. For example, people have noted the increase in the degree of liberalism of the New York Times over time.

<u>Policy</u>

Thus far we have examined behavioral propositions. The great divide explains so many otherwise inexplicable features of political behavior. That suggests that it can also provide insight into policy questions. To move from behavioral propositions to propositions about desirable policy, it is necessary to have some notion about what constitutes good policy. For the most part philosophers either assert that it cannot be done without arbitrary assumptions or they are willing to make assumptions that others regard as arbitrary. Instead, I start with a simple, common sense idea – that is good which people would want if they had enough information. In Chapter 6 I provide a more elaborate defense of that idea, but it corresponds to what many use implicitly when they write about policy. People are free to accept that goal or not, but I suspect that that goal is acceptable. Who would want something other than what they want? Who would deny that they could make better choices with better information?

That goal by itself leads to no policy preferences. Indeed, that is one of its virtues. Arguments over appropriate policy become arguments over empirical propositions which can be settled by evidence. The goal also provides one of the ways to gather the appropriate evidence. One of the differences between actual and desirable choices is produced by better information.

The focus of this book is on the impact of better information on choices as long as voters regard that information as relevant to their voting decision.

There is such a thing as innate human nature, the satisfying of which creates good policy. However, there are several innate preferences that sometimes conflict, most particularly self-interest and altruism. But there is a barrier to achieving an individual's most desirable combination of these two preferences, and that is limited information. Increasing information, holding costs constant, should improve policy.

One of the biggest barriers to knowledge acquisition is confirmation bias. In particular, liberal altruists are, for the most part, naïve altruists. They refuse to recognize the unintended unfavorable consequences of their liberal altruistic proposals. One of the reasons for this bias is that one's friends are similarly naïve. Nevertheless, taking unintended consequences seriously causes some of the previously liberal altruists to change their policy views. This book provides some evidence of this phenomenon.

Confirmation bias is a characteristic of all humans, conservatives and liberals alike. But conservatives are more focused on self-interest, and people have better information about what constitutes their own self-interest, and so are less subject to confirmation bias in their decisions. Furthermore, the usual liberal intended consequences of government policy are likely to be known to conservatives whether they like it or not.

Even with enough information, there would be considerable disagreement about what constitutes good policy. What is required is some way to aggregate political preferences. There is considerable agreement about the appropriate way to do this: the democratic ideal, where the interests of each member of the polity is given equal weight. Representative democracy with the rule of law is generally considered the best approximation to this ideal even though all recognize the problems associated with that approximation.

Our best guess at what constitutes good policy would be those policies that would be adopted in a democracy if all the participants had enough information. That guess is also the guess of virtually all of the political scientists who focus on the information problems in democratic governance, for example Althaus, 2001. Their whole concern is the extent that lack of political information interferes with the democratic ideal, an ideal that they share. From our examination of the impact of information on the preferences of naïve altruists, we know that there would be fewer liberal altruists if naïve altruists became less naïve. Then, the policy preferences of these liberal altruists would be given less weight in democratic decisions. In consequence, policy would become less liberal with greater information.

More speculatively, the impact of the democratic ideal on altruistic voting could be even greater than that. The democratic ideal is a policy goal. As such, it would appear to be what altruists would seek with full information as the criterion for good policy. It would then act as the full information substitute for the goals of naïve altruism. If that were the case, democratic decision making would boil down to an aggregation of self-interested and traditional voting. The altruists would accede to those decisions because they were democratic decisions.

This implication of the democratic ideal as the sole guide to policy turns a standard philosophic procedure on its head. To determine the social good philosophers have insisted that one looks only at impartial decisions, for the obvious reason that any one person's policy judgment is affected by his own self-interest. It is not just philosophers who recognize this self-interested bias. Nearly everybody condemns the role of "special interests" in determining government policy. That amounts to condemning the impact of a small group of self-interested individuals on policy. That condemnation arises out of the democratic ideal in which the interests of everybody are given equal weight in policy decisions. I argue in the rest of this book that the "special interest" phenomenon is not as crucial as the "great divide" in determining policy outcomes on the issues on which this book focuses, though special interest produces problems of its own. In consequence, the self-interested component of democratic decisions about our issues is an aggregation of the self-interest of the bulk of voters. The argument that self-interested decisions bias individual decision making has less force in condemning self-interest when one is talking about the aggregation of those self-interested decisions across the whole electorate. As a first approximation, that aggregation eliminates the bias and is all we have together with traditionalism, given the sole force of the democratic ideal on altruism.

But it is unreasonable to expect altruists to make the democratic ideal their sole value. As discussed in Chapter 7, people tend to give greater weight to policy consequences than to the processes that generate those consequences even though those processes have important long term consequences of their own. But concern with processes carries some weight in political decisions. In consequence, we would expect some substitution of the democratic ideal for the other goals of altruism. Since that substitution does not occur in naïve altruism, we would expect naïve altruism to play a lesser role in political decisions with some recognition of the democratic ideal.

This argument cannot be successfully countered by the assertion that the rich have an undue influence on redistributive decisions. On the surface this argument would appear to have some force given the democratic ideal of equal weight to the interest of each person. I show in this book, however, that in spite of their greater influence on government decisions in general, the rich do not have greater influence on decisions concerned with redistribution from the rich in general to the poor in general. After all, the redistribution that occurs in a democracy is from rich to poor. The rich as individuals have other fish to fry. One of the manifestations of the other interests of many specific rich persons is their advocacy of assorted special interest legislation. This produces the serious problem of corporate welfare, but is not relevant to the issues examined in this book. The groups that do have a more than proportional influence on redistributive decisions are educators and the media. These groups are not simply dispassionate distributors of truth. Chapter 3 details the liberal bias of educators independently of any knowledge they possess and how that bias is transmitted to the media.

The policy proposals in this book are feasible. They do

not require converting the self-interested into altruists or the reverse. Nor do they demand that voters acquire more information when it is not in their interest. All that is demanded is an educational reform: to have educators' discussion of policy include discussions of unintended consequences and the implications of the competitive ideal. Given the current nature of the educational system, that might be considered a tall order, but even some minor change in that direction would be useful. This reform does not even require more information, but rather a substitution of information relevant for voter decisions for much of the irrelevant information now being taught.

The purpose of this Overview is to provide a road map to the arguments contained in the rest of the book. It is short of both analysis and evidence because that is the essence of what follows.

CHAPTER 2

SELF-INTEREST, TRADITIONS AND NAÏVE ALTRUISM

Self-Interest

Most economic analyses of the political process focus on self-interest, for example, Stigler (1971), Becker (1983), Peltzman (1980), and Weeden and Kurtzban (2014). Indeed, those analyses have had some success. Votes for Republicans increase with income. Union members and welfare recipients tend to vote for Democrats by a greater amount than their incomes would have predicted. But self-interest variables are not the most important variables determining political preferences (Nelson and Greene, 2003). For example, in 2012, those with annual incomes greater than $180,000 showed barely more support for Romney than those with incomes from $120,000 to $180,000 (Gallup, 2012).

There is a reason for this relatively less important role of self-interest in determining votes. The simple self-interest model for voting has a serious problem, a problem pointed out by Buchanan (1980) and others a long time ago. In the large group setting of the typical election, a voter has a negligible effect on election outcomes. In consequence, his vote has virtually no impact on the consequences that flow from those outcomes. His self-interest is not seriously affected by his vote.

It is remarkable that, in spite of this phenomenon, self-interest does seem to affect people's votes. However, one would expect that effect to be considerably muted compared to the way self-interest affects market decisions, where an individual's decisions can have significant consequences to that individual.

Some explanation is required for the role of self-interest in voting at all. One can think of voting preferences as an extension of policy preferences expressed in conversations. The secret ballot does not usually produce a discrepancy between votes and expressed opinions, especially to friends. That would be considered hypocrisy, and people would prefer not to be accused of that sin. When one expresses a political preference among friends, he does not expect that opinion to directly affect policy outcomes. It is just talk because people like to talk. The variables that produce political talk are the same variables that increase voter participation. For example, those people who read newspapers more frequently and those people with strong political opinions are more likely to vote (Nelson and Greene, 2003).

Self-interested concerns do affect political opinions expressed in conversations even though they as individuals cannot affect the outcome of elections. This is especially true if the conversations are with friends with the same self-interest. One votes those self-interested concerns and any other concerns that arise in those conversations. For example, coal mining country was particularly opposed to Democrats in the 2016 election because of the Democrats anti-coal policy.

Why would a citizen bother with the voting extension of conversation? Voting involves some cost and no individual voter affects outcomes. This is the paradox of voting that has long been discussed in the literature. The most obvious explanation is that it is considered "good" to vote and people want to be considered "good" by others and themselves. As evidence that voting is considered "good", there are frequent public service announcements from non-partisan sources urging people to vote. Charitable contributions are also motivated by a desire to be "good" and seen to be "good". As some evidence that "goodness" motivations help determine voting participation, the variables that determine charitable contributions also determine voting participation in the same direction (Nelson and Greene, 2003).

Another voting motivator is the joy of participation in a well-publicized activity. There is a consumption return to being part of a group activity. That is part of the motivation for the participation in demonstrations and riots.

It is instructive to compare governmental elections with other kinds of elections. Fans vote in All Star elections in Major League Baseball in spite of the fact that they have nothing material to gain by doing so and that their individual vote has no significant effect on that election's outcome. They do get, however, the joy of participation in a well-publicized group activity. They talk about who the baseball stars are and their vote is just a continuation of that conversation.

In contrast, the fact that the small individual investor has no impact on elections for Corporate Board Members is the dominant determinant of the non-voting behavior of those investors unless proxy battlers make voting virtually cost free by telephoning those investors. Small investors are neither considered "good" by voting nor do they get any pleasure in participating with a group of friends. Furthermore, they probably spend little time talking about management performance in the stocks that they own.

One of the most obvious competitors to self-interest in conversation is gossip, discussions about personal characteristics of the gossip's subjects. Often that gossip is focused on the subject's disapproved sexual behavior. When that conversation focuses on politicians, it often affects voting way out of proportion to the consequences of that inappropriate sexual behavior on any policy effects of that politician in office. Such sexual gossip is fun and so would generate more conversation than more serious discussions of policy. Declines in Donald Trumps' poll numbers as evidence of his sexual proclivities were revealed strongly suggest that non-policy concerns do affect voting when they affect conversation. This is evidence that voting preferences are an extension of conversational preferences. Gossip based voting is probably the clearest evidence for conversation based voting precisely because the consequences of sexual misconduct on the policy choices of the miscreant are minute.

In summary, there is a self-interest effect on voting choices in governmental elections, but it is a muted effect. Given the muted self-interest effect on voting choices, one would expect other determinants of voting behavior to play important roles. Schuessler (2000), Congleton (2007). and Carlsson and Johanson-Stenman (2010) provide evidence that beliefs or social norms play a central role in determining voter decisions. They call this expressive voting. However, without knowing more about the character of these norms, the expressive voter approach provides limited insight into voter behavior. I shall examine how these norms operate.

My position is that these social norms affect behavior because voters want to be considered good and to consider themselves good. There is, indeed, a self-interest component in this desire because the attitudes of others toward a person have important consequences to that person. The attitudes of others are affected by the political position a person adopts, but are not affected by whether the policy that person advocates is realized or not. In consequence, the return to goodness is not subject to the large group problem. Thus it will be greater relative to narrow self-interest for voter decisions compared to market decisions.[1]

Not all of goodness can be attributed to self-interest. One of the elements of goodness is a conscience or how one views oneself. A person is interested in choosing good political positions in part to satisfy himself. Though Nelson and Greene (2003) have shown how a conscience is usually consistent with genetic survival, it will often lead to behavior that is inconsistent with what is usually regarded as self-interest. The standard view of conscience is that it is an internalization of what others regard as appropriate behavior (Coleman 1990)—what others would think about one's behavior if they knew about it. Though they might not know about a person's behavior today, they are likely to find out about it in the future, much to the disadvantage of bad actors. But individual decisions are often myopic in that they give less weight to long run consequences than genetic survival would require. A conscience is an imperfect way correcting for that myopia.

Conscience plays an important role in voter decisions. There is a conscience cost in being a hypocrite, saying one thing while doing another. Even though others do not observe a person's vote, they do observe a person's verbalized political position. Because of the free rider problem, there is virtually no return to a person voting differently than he talks, and there is the conscience cost of hypocrisy. Hence the usual success of polls in predicting voting behavior, though sometimes voters talk differently to pollsters than they do to their friends.

Imitation

Probably, the most important way a voter achieves social approval is by imitating the assertions of others about their votes. That imitation signals to others that the voter wants their approval. The incentive to imitate is particularly strong if those others are the people with whom the voter wants future relationships. This signal works because others rightly interpret a person's vote that way. A vote opposed to those of his previous friendship group is a strike against continued friendship, sometimes a fatal strike.

This desire to imitate is probably something more than a conscious rational decision. It has generated such a significant return to humans that it has become a built in preference—a preference to conform. This conforming preference is so strong that it affects behavior even when the person to whom one is conforming is in no position to help or harm the conformer.

This behavior sometimes leads to polling error when voters speak differently to pollsters than they do to their friends. This occurs when voters believe that pollsters would prefer a different response than do their friends because voters believe that pollsters are more politically correct. Nelson and Greene (2003) cite two such cases. In the 1989 New York City mayoralty race between the white, Guiliani, and the black, Dinkins, the forecast vote for the latter was 12 to 16 percent higher than his actual vote. In the 1990 Louisiana senatorial race featuring David Duke, of KKK fame, Duke's actual vote was 19 percent higher than his forecast vote. The desire to be considered good by pollsters was enough to overcome the hypocrisy charge, even though pollsters were not in position to benefit or harm the respondent. This charge was somewhat muted by polls asking voters how they will vote, an answer that can be different than the actual vote. In the New York City case the difference between exit polls and actual votes was less than the difference between actual votes and forecast votes. The former case involved actual lying, though even in this case the difference continued to exist. Some people believe that in the

2016 presidential election's polls, the underestimation of the support for Donald Trump was attributable to the same process.

Asch (1969) provides evidence for the influence of others even when the others are clearly wrong. A substantially larger group of people denied the evidence before their eyes—large differences in the length of lines on a piece of paper—when all others denied such evidence in their presence than when none denied it (32 percent compared to 1 percent). The Asch case resembles political choice in one important respect. In both cases there are no serious costs to the individual in the consequences of truth denial.

As important as imitation is to voting, it does not by itself determine how a person votes. That clearly depends upon how others vote. If that voter and others determined their votes by their own self-interest and imitation, the resulting vote would be determined by a weighted aggregation of the self-interest of the imitative group, a conclusion demonstrated in Nelson and Greene (2003).

Many of the imitative group have similar self-interests as the voter. As a result, imitation will have a multiplier effect on the voter's own self-interest in determining his vote. His vote will be partially determined by his self-interest and the similar self-interest of his friends. But most voters are not certain about all the policy differences between candidates and how those differences affect their own self-interest. Given this lack of information, they might choose to imitate people outside their group, especially if they believe those outsiders to be more knowledgeable—educators and the media in particular. This imitation makes a lot of sense if the political process is not simply a zero sum game. In that case, it pays to imitate anybody whose interests are not opposed to one's own if one feels that they know more.

Traditionalism

There is an important behavior that amounted to imitation of one's associates in the distant past but is not quite imitating them now. People use as their guide to appropriate behavior current policies and policies of the recent past. Hunter-gatherer societies in which most of man's innate preferences were being formed, were relatively homogeneous. The social rules prevailing in any group were the social rules approved by one's associates. In consequence, accepting those social rules was the way to gain social acceptance from those who counted. Now, of course, social rules are formed by the impact of many people, only a few of whom are people whom one knows. But nonetheless people use those social rules in determining what is appropriate. That tendency is considerably fortified by the knowledge that one's friends are using those social rules as determinants of appropriate rules, so by using this rule one is in affect imitating one's friends.

This approval of existing rules makes sense on other grounds as well. The fact that these rules have survived means that the societies with those rules has survived (Hayek,1988). Social rules that include traditionalism are more likely to survive than the same set of rules without the rule that produces traditionalism.

Of course, traditionalism downplays innovation. Innovation of social rules is a mixed bag. If it were simply random, one would expect its expected results to be unfavorable at least in the short run. But innovation can be purposive in a way that improves group survival. But, as we shall show, that is not always the case, so traditionalism survives.

This use of group survival makes evolutionary sense given the substantial individual survival returns to imitating others. When it pays for individuals to imitate the group, group survival can help determine individual characteristics, in particular, the characteristic of supporting existing rules.

There has been considerable dispute in the evolutionary biology literature over whether it is group survival or individual survival that determines the course of evolution. However, when individual survival is contingent upon group approval, the two can yield the same results unless there are other processes that generate a conflict. When it comes to verbal approval of current social rules, there does not seem to be such a conflict. Behaviorally, accepting all the social rules is another story. Sexual relations in conflict with social norms can be such a case.

Froehlich et al. (1987) ran an interesting experiment that demonstrated the effect of political positions of strangers on one's own political position. They were interested in determining the values people used in evaluating policy. They found that the values respondents initially proposed were modified when they found out what values others proposed even though they did not know the others. The modification was to adopt the average position of these others. When one as well as others know little about appropriate rules, the average of everybody's view is likely to be better than one's own uninformed view.

In hunter-gatherer societies, the social rules changed only slowly so using prevailing social rules in one's youth would also suffice as a way to win friends. One learned appropriate social rules while one was young. Now, of course, social rules change considerably over time. But youthful learning of social rules still has an impact in determining what people think are appropriate social rules. Again, that tendency is reinforced if one's friends and associates are also using past social rules in determining appropriate behavior. Nelson and Greene (2003) found that the region in which one was born had approximately the same effect on political positions as the region of current residence.

This dependence on the status quo in the present and the recent past has a similar role as imitation. Neither process by itself predicts political positions. They are endogenous variables. They depend on the political positions taken by others without fully determining those positions. If self-interest were the only other determinant of political positions, the political position of people would be a function of one's own self-interest and the self-interest of others. But self-interest is not the only determinant of traditional views. As previously discussed, group survival is also a relevant determinant of traditions

Hayek rightly claims that free-markets developed in spite of popular views against such trade. Inter-tribal trade provided a free-market niche in the social rules. Those rules specified the interchanges between tribal members and the resulting intra-tribal exchanges. But inter-tribal trade was not subjected to the rules governing intra-tribal exchanges. Ofek (2001) makes a distinction between nepotistic exchange and mercantile exchange. In the former, exchanges were governed by rules that emphasized interpersonal relationships rather than the value of the things exchanged. Mercantile exchange reversed that emphasis. Intra-tribal relationships were more easily subjected to rules than intertribal interactions, so mercantile exchange could more easily developed in the latter.

But intertribal exchanges had to overcome xenophobia. What was required was the substantial private return to engage in such trade and the greater survival of groups that did not prohibit that trade. Xenophobia could be strong enough in some tribes to prevent inter-tribal trade, but all that is necessary is that it wasn't strong enough in some tribes to allow those tribes to trade. The survival advantages of such trade were sufficiently strong that the tribes that allowed such trade eventually became the dominant tribes. These tribes need not actively encouraged such trade as long as they allowed it. The self-interest of the traders would take care of the rest.

In the case of free trade the individuals within the tribe benefited so group survival occurred by way of the self-interest of members of the group. The crucial characteristic that Hayek emphasizes is that this benefit to individuals does not require that they know they are benefited. Voting on the grounds of tradition can be a substitute for informed self-interested voting.

Altruism

Self-interest and the wish to imitate are innate preferences – individual preferences that are part of human nature. They exist in all cultures. But there are other relevant universal preferences that are regarded as innate by most scholars such as Haidt (2012) and Boehm (2012): in particular, altruism. They provide some evidence for that position such as babies responding to the need of others long before they are socialized to do so. The same areas of the brain that are activated when one smiles are activated when one observes others smiling. This empathy has an evolutionary return. It increases cooperative behavior. There is a self-interested return in reciprocal long term relationships. In terms of game theory, playing tit for tat is a winning strategy, but it is not clear that the initial tat is always a winning move. Empathy increases the probability of that cooperative beginning. Empathy also enables a person to forecast the intentions of others by putting himself in their place (Zak, 2011). That the brain is built to increase cooperative behavior is suggested by animal studies. Even some species of monkeys are willing to forego food in order to punish conspecifics who violated sharing norms (Zak, 2011). That occurs even when their self-interest is to eat. This suggests that at least part of empathy is innate.

Most people agree that there is an altruistic component to charity. An important determinant of a success of a charity is how effectively it convinces would-be donors that it promotes social ideals. Currently, a lot of charity focuses on expenditures on the environment, education, health, the poor, and assorted cultural activities.

But private charity is not the only source of funds for those purposes. There can also be government expenditures. Advocating greater government expenditures for these purposes is the essence of the liberal agenda. The other large category of charitable contribution is contributions to religious institutions. These contributions are not associated with liberals. One possible explanation is that liberals tend to be non-religious. I will call the voting thus produced "liberal altruistic voting."

I will argue in the ensuing pages that liberal altruistic voting and the imitation of liberal altruistic voters are important determinants of voting positions. Liberal altruists want governments to do what charities do, the essence of the liberal political position. In consequence, this tends to make the combination of other determinants of voting more conservative in comparison. Obviously, there are groups whose self-interest is seemingly benefited by greater government expenditures as they are currently distributed. But in combination with traditional voting, the self-interested aggregate must be more conservative than liberal altruism. This self-interested aggregation is determined by the aggregation of self-interested voting in a polity.

The leap from private charity to liberal altruistic voting is quite a leap. First of all, altruistic voting is subject to the same large group problem as self-interested voting. One's vote has little impact on the consequences of elections because it has little impact on election results. But self-interest still affects elections, and so does altruism and for the same underlying reason. People sometimes talk about what they think is good for society. That voting as an extension of conversation means that votes will sometimes be influenced by voters' views of the social good.

Liberal altruistic voting differs from charitable contributions in that no direct sacrifice is required for that voting preference. Indeed, the non-consequential impact of a person's political position might make it easier to cast altruistic votes. They are, at first glance, cost free. If they generate a warm glow anyhow, an altruistic voter is ahead of the game. This is quite different from charitable contributions that involve real sacrifices. It is not surprising under those circumstances that charitable contributions and liberal altruistic voting have substantially different effects on the attitude of others toward a person. Charitable contributions are admired by nearly everybody even when those contributions are different than their own. They appropriately signal that a person would make a good reciprocity partner. (Nelson and Green, 2003). They enhance a person's reputation universally whether they are designed to do so or not. In contrast, liberal altruistic voting mainly enhances a person's reputation among the like-minded. It is not reputation enhancing among those with opposite political preferences. Liberal altruistic voting mainly signals just the opposite to those with different political preferences, that a person so voting would not be a good reciprocity partner for them.

But the effect of a person's liberal altruistic voting on people's attitudes has some similarity to the effects of charity. They both are generated by conversations about the social good. The derogatory label attached to liberal altruistic voters by their antagonists is "do-gooders", the mildest of pejoratives.

It is a recognition that liberal altruistic voters' motives are good even when one disagrees with their policies. This is a recognition that liberal altruistic voters in turn do not accord to other voters, who are often regarded by the former as evil incarnate. This difference in attitudes toward the other political party has been noted fairly frequently by others such as Charles Krautheimer. Some call it virtue signaling on the part of Democrats. The Democratic view of Republicans explains the results of a survey done by Yougov in September 2016, which showed that 87 percent of would be Clinton voters believed that at least half of would be Trump voters were racists, the word de jour for "evil". There is an interesting quote from Nancy Pelosi, The Speaker of the House of Representatives (O'Neil, 1017): "Democrats do the Lord's work while Republicans dishonor God". This is a rather curious way to claim the moral superiority of Democrats who are significantly less religious than Republicans.

Sowell (2009) makes the same distinction between what liberal altruists think of themselves and the self-evaluation of others, but he and the others do not explain why there is such a distinction when being a liberal altruistic voter is cost-free.

"If you happen to believe in free markets, judicial restraint, traditional values and other features of the tragic vision, then you are someone who believes in free markets, judicial restraint and traditional values. There is no personal exaltation resulting from those beliefs. But to be for "social justice" and "saving the environment", or to be "anti-war" is more than just a set of beliefs about empirical facts. This vision puts you on a higher moral plane as someone concerned and compassionate, someone who is for peace in the world, a defender of the downtrodden, and someone who wants to preserve the beauty of nature and save the planet from being polluted by others less caring. In short, one vision makes you somebody special and the other vision does not.

This cost-free moral high ground of liberal altruists has impacts. Though people are more interested in what their friends think about them than the thoughts of others, the thoughts of others make some difference. Everybody would like to wrap their political position in the mantle of altruism. That wrap also improves their evaluation of themselves. Haidt (2012) finds that reasoned defenses of political positions are mostly rationalizations of those positions rather than the bases of those positons. But that is an easier sell for some political positions rather than others. The distinction between altruistic positions and self-interested positions is not in whether a group is using an altruistic rationale or not. It is in whether they can sell that position to others on altruistic grounds. For example, much charity is motivated by compassion. Blacks and women can use the compassion argument to further their political agenda. There usually is some basis for those demands that could help convince others. On average Blacks and women make less than others. But their programs confer benefits on the non-poor as well. Affirmative Action is not a program for the exclusive benefit of the poor. Similarly, those interested in outdoor activities-- the Sierra Club and the Audubon Society, for example-- are in the forefront of advocating more expenditures or regulation to keep the environment "pristine". But they are joined by many couch potatoes who are convinced that "saving" the environment is moral as witnessed by charitable contributions for that purpose. A defense of the free-market is a harder sell on altruistic grounds because it more clearly has self-interest benefits.

As a result of the failure of the conservative's altruistic sell, one would expect them to be more tolerant of moral liberals than liberals of immoral conservatives. After all, liberal causes are judged to be moral causes, while conservative causes are not so regarded. That can affect businesses which have customers across the ideological spectrum. They can be threatened with boycotts from would be customers in response to political contributions which bother some customers enough. The evidence suggests that liberals are more likely to use the boycott weapon than conservatives. The Wall Street Journal reported the plight of conservative talk radio (February 4, 2015). "Radio executives said the erosion of add dollars from talk stations was driven in part by a series of organized media campaigns in early 2012 that scared away advertisers." The greater liberal use of boycotts is the most obvious explanation for Democrats support for and Republican opposition to full disclosure of business political contributions, which would reveal firms that could be targeted by boycotts.

Part of the greater use of boycotts by liberals can be explained by the nature of liberalism, skepticism about the efficacy of free-markets. PETA, for example, has an aversion to products made of fur. Conservatives by nature have less to complain about the products freely chosen by consumers. Similarly, the pro-union stance of liberals increases their support for union originated boycotts. But even when we just count boycotts that are political in nature, liberals are more likely to engage in boycotts than conservatives. In its list of notable boycotts, Wikepedia lists many more politically oriented boycotts for liberal groups than conservative groups: fourteen to two (Wikepedia, 2016). (A curious feature of that list is that half of reported liberal political boycotts were organized by LGBT groups. That category of boycotts is one where both liberals and conservatives can make a moral argument for their support of boycotts.)

There is another consequence of liberals possessing the moral high road. With felt morality on his side, a person is more willing to advertise his political position. Nelson and Greene (2003) found that in the first three months of 1998 the New York Times reported eighteen anti-market demonstrations and zero pro-market demonstrations. The former were demonstrations against poverty, unemployment, and market induced price increases and in favor of environmental causes. The latter would have been demonstrations against increases in the role of government relative to the market. It is significant that in 1998 there was a Democratic president, a fact which would have made liberal demonstrations somewhat less likely because there was less for them to object to as far as government policy was concerned. The later demonstrations associated with the Tea Party are an exception to these results, but would still be overwhelmed by the sheer number of liberal demonstrations from Occupy Wall Street to Black Lives Matter.

Liberal Altruism

Not all altruistic voters are liberals. There are altruistic reasons to condemn the policies of the liberal altruistic voter. Adam Smith, for example, believed that free markets were the most desirable of anti-poverty programs and so would object on altruistic grounds to the liberal agenda which reduces the role of free-markets. A lot of evidence has accumulated since his time to strongly support that characteristic of free-markets at least as far as long-run consequences are concerned.

Many of the empirical results, especially those of Chapter 3, suggest that this non-liberal altruism does not dominate in determining the votes of most conservatives. It is self-interest and traditionalism combined with imitation that play the important roles in determining conservatives' political preferences. Haidt (2012) presents some relevant evidence. He finds that his measure of altruism is a less important criterion determining conservative votes than liberal votes.

In spite of the fact that liberal altruism is only one form of altruism, it dominates the intellectual world. Why? The very nature of social ideals – liberal or religious – is to object to some forms of narrow self-interested behavior. No social ideal is required for the promotion of narrow self-interest even when it is socially beneficial. That is what people would do with or without a social norm to make them do it. A defense of narrow self-interest arises only to counter arguments to the contrary: Adam Smith vs. the mercantilists for example

In hunter-gatherer societies the focus of economic social rules centered on the requirements of cooperation, especially those associated with big game hunting. Society condemned those who did not engage in food sharing of big game or those who malingered in the hunt (Boehm, 2012). Food sharing of big game and condemnations of malingering in the hunt were the rules. At the same time, hunter gatherers did not share in food gathering and small game. But there was no real rule that this self-interested behavior be allowed. That behavior occurred without rules. In consequence, the social rules focused on the evils of greed, i.e. self-interest, even though greedy behavior, self-interest, was accepted as appropriate in certain contexts.

Even today there is general agreement about some conditions where greed is bad. There are a wide range of criminal acts that people agree should be considered criminal. But there is substantial disagreement about the greed associated with free markets. The invisible hand is, indeed, invisible to many.

Charity is an attempt to rectify by private action some of the consequences of greed. Why shouldn't the same activities be pursued by government? People admire others who give to charity in part because the admirers do not have to bear the costs. The liberal altruistic voter tends to ignore the costs of governmental charity as well, though he is one of the cost bearers in this case. However, he is happiest when he can redistribute the costs to others: the "rich" in particular.

It does appear that the liberal altruistic voter's default position is a condemnation of the greed associated with free-markets. There is an example of that attitude incorporated into law. The employees of government and non-profits are treated more favorably than others when it comes to paying back student loans even when income is held constant. Evidently, their activities are considered worthier than the greedy behavior associated with standard markets.

The direct problems associated with those markets are clearly visible, particularly the poverty of the poor or air pollution. Condemnations of this behavior is easy. This condemnation contrasts with the dominance of free-markets in our economy, a dominance that has a substantial effect on traditionalists. Traditionalists will usually take the side of self-interested voters even though current policies have been partially determined by liberal altruistic voters. The reason: the proportion of GDP devoted to domestic government expenditures and the amount of government regulation has increased over time. Those voting for the present and past state of the world will be voting against this increase in the role of government. That puts them together with the aggregate of self-interested voters on the opposite side of liberal altruists. This conflict is the source of a great voter divide.

This divide is a gulf, but probably not a yawning gulf. Some people can be only partially liberal altruistic voters. Furthermore, liberal altruistic voting affects voting outcomes in both the past and the present. So the status quo is affected by liberal altruistic voters, and thus affecting the preferences of traditionalists. And, of course, most liberal altruistic voters are also affected to a lesser degree by their own self-interest and the status quo, though that latter effect is quite different than the effect for other voters.

The status quo affects the way most voters perceive policy issues. People are asked in polls if the government should spend more, the same, or less on welfare, the environment etc.

Traditionalists would answer such questions by choosing "the same" or "less" because these expenditures have grown over time. Self-interested voters would, on average, be likely to do the same because liberal altruists have influenced current government policy to make government expenditures greater than the aggregate of self-interested voters would prefer. Liberal altruistic voters would answer, "more", because this is a way of showing one is on the side of the angels. All of these answers do not require even a foggiest idea about what are the appropriate levels of expenditures. The answers are still enough to tell oneself and others what side one is on. That low information requirement probably is also characteristic of most political conversations.

Problems with Liberal Altruism

There are lots of problems with liberal altruistic voting in our own culture. We know little through personal contact about most of our fellow members of a polity. In consequence, we have to depend on the words of others, particularly the media and educators.

The evolutionary roots of altruism are associated with helping children, the needy, and the sick. But by way of educators and the media contemporary liberal altruism can extend way beyond those roots. When it does, its policy goals become even less precise. There is considerable disagreement among naïve altruists as to what their goals should be.

For example, all other things being equal, naïve altruists want to protect wildlife but that by itself does not generate predictions about how naïve altruists would vote. When it came to DDT, they wanted it banned to protect eagles in particular in spite of that ban increasing human deaths by way of increases in malaria. But when it came to wind turbines naïve altruists are mostly in favor of them in spite of the many birds including eagles that these turbines kill. Part of that difference in behavior is an information problem, which effect gets publicized. But part is attributable to the fuzziness of altruism itself.

Currently, altruism has been extended toward baby seals, whales, and Bambi deer. PETA demands that animals be treated as if they were humans. Though PETA's membership is limited, its attitude in somewhat muted form has had enough of an impact to affect legislation. The Endangered Species act seeks what its advocates regard as environmental protection through preservation of animal (and plant) species. Gallup found that 32 percent of those surveyed in the United States believed that animals should have the same rights as people as opposed to having some rights. Many naïve altruists would disagree with the former.

There is a certain pattern to social ideals as they manifest themselves in charitable contributions. Environmental expenditures probably had their origins in concerns about externalities: costs or benefits that are not properly considered in market decisions because they affect people not involved in those decisions. But those origins hardly explain the current environmental movement. Even moderate environmentalists, such as Farber (1999), believe that nature has values beyond its value to man. Nobel laureate Sen (2001) asserts that environmental benefits to man should be given greater weight in governmental decisions than other benefits. Indeed, this disconnect between externality correction and environmentalism is even manifest in the environmentalist definition of what constitutes a good environment. Instead of the obvious, "the environment that man would want if he had enough information," all sorts of oddities creep up. There is Wilson's (1992) view: that a good environment is one which maximizes the number of species or the view of others that that environment is best which minimizes man's footprint. Nor are these views eccentricities of fringe groups. They are sufficiently influential to have an impact on government policy. For example, the Environmental Protection Agency maintained that it did not have to consider costs under The Clean Air Act, a position struck down by a 2015 ruling of the Supreme Court (Wall Street Journal, 2015). Without cost considerations environmental purity becomes the sole criterion for policy, a position that makes no sense unless environmental quality is an end in itself.

Some ideals, of course, do seem to have their origins in self-interest. "Women's rights" advocates are more likely to be women than men. Outdoor organizations are in the forefront of the environmental movement. But proponents of these ideals are not confined to the self-serving. Their appeal goes far beyond such limits.

Another charitable theme is compassion that has been extended beyond aid to the poor, the sick, and children to concerns about women, poorer ethnic groups, and animals. It is likely that there is a biologic base for some form of compassion, addressed toward one's more unfortunate associates and children of those associates. But among many in some societies there appears to be a tendency to extend compassion far beyond that basis. This generalizing tendency far beyond innate preferences is exemplified by Rawls' (1971) difference principle: maximize the wellbeing of the least fortunate. As Froehlich et al. (1987) have demonstrated, that is not the principle of justice that most people accept. They looked at people's views on justice both before and after discussing those views with their fellow respondents. In neither case was the Rawls' principle of justice the preferred view.

These extensions of altruism beyond its original meaning makes the concept somewhat ambiguous. Altruism implies a desire to help others, but which others? People disagree on whether they feel they are citizens of the world, their country, or their locality. They disagree on the extent they should be concerned with future generations long in the future. These disagreements are not just disagreements between people, but many people are so uncertain of the dimensions of altruism that they can change their view if the questions that elicit their views are rephrased or if others influence them as in the Froehlich case above.

Confirmation Bias

The more serious problem with liberal altruistic voting is naivete. In the small group setting of hunter-gatherers, people knew the extent to which need could be attributed to laziness or malingering. Altruism was adjusted by equity—that returns should be proportional to inputs. Boehm (2012) and Haidt

(2012) believe that equity in the sense of rewards in proportion to inputs was also an innate preference. That equity adjustment made efficiency sense. There is a disincentive effect of aid to the needy. Aid to the needy makes them less needy, and, thereby decreases their incentive to reduce their neediness on their own. "Why not stay needy and continue to receive the largesse of others?" Focusing aid to those who are needy through no fault of their own, considerably reduces that problem. Many of the sick and children are the most obvious examples of no-fault need, and, hence, less likely to escape their need on their own.

In a large society, most of whose members are not known to others, correcting aid to the needy for its disincentive effects is not easy. Most people find out about disincentive effects either through reading or by what others say. Those activities are avoidable if one chooses. One can choose not to read such material and not to associate with people who talk about disincentive effects. And liberal altruists have an incentive to so choose. In addition to the desire to associate with people of similar beliefs, there is the well-known confirmation bias. One wants to hear only that which confirms one's political position. The likelihood of encountering information about disincentive effects is minimal for liberal altruists who associate primarily with other liberal altruists. Discussions of these disincentive effects of aid to the needy are common, but not among liberal altruistic voters and the media and educators they encounter. Because of this largely absent concern with unintended consequences of the policies they advocate, liberal altruistic voters can justifiably be called naïve altruists. Haidt (2012) finds that most responses to moral and political questions are emotional responses with a minimum of thoughtful analysis, and that thoughtful analysis is largely a rationalization of those responses rather than the source of them. That kind of response makes ignoring contrary information particularly easy. This ignoring of unintended consequences has been noted also by Foster (2014).

Confirmation bias is a two way street. It is a characteristic of all humans whether liberal or conservative. Jerit and Barabas (2012) show that Democrats and Republicans show very similar tendencies to ignore uncomfortable political facts and to remember comfortable facts.

There are, however, two reasons why confirmation bias has a more important effect on liberals in political decisions. First, self-interest is a bigger component of conservatives' political decisions. People have a greater incentive to avoid confirmation bias when making their own market decisions. If a person gets his information to aid market decisions, he will have that information when he is making his political decisions. Coal miners are likely to know how they are affected by the EPA's Clean Power Act, for example. It makes a difference in any decisions to migrate or educate their children.

Second, in a period when government expenditures on domestic programs are increasing, a substantial portion of the desirable effects of legislation are contained in its direct effects. For example, it would be hard for a conservative voter who knew that there was a legislative proposal to increase the minimum wage not to know that the legislation would increase the minimum wage. It would be a lot easier for a liberal voter not to know that there were employment effects of that minimum wage legislation.

Because of confirmation bias, the timing of events is important. Suppose a person's desire to aid the needy arises before the opportunity to learn of the disincentive effects of that aid. Then, it is less likely that that person will learn of those effects. The innate character of altruism suggests that that is, indeed, the order of events.

Presently, there are many ways that the disincentive effect of aid to the needy can manifest itself. Aid to the poor can discourage education by increasing the income of the uneducated. It can encourage single motherhood with a consequent reduction in investment in children. Both impacts of welfare have serious consequences on poverty in the next generation. Not only do welfare payments increase the potential income of single mothers, it also reduces the cost to other family members if one of their family unit becomes a single mother. This reduces the family pressure not to become a single mother. Single motherhood via aid to the poor directly reduces investment in children quality. Conard (2016) shows an enormous effect of marriage on the ability of the next generation to escape poverty. About 50 percent of the children in unmarried households in the lowest income quintile remained in that quintile when adult. In contrast, about 18 percent of children from married households in that income quantile remained as adults in that lowest quantile.

Unemployment insurance, one response to the needy, reduces migration in search of a job, since it reduces the cost of not having a job. Why move to North Dakota where jobs are plentiful when friends are plentiful where one is?

One could argue that aid to the needy has long run, indirect beneficial effects through productive consumption. It is conceivable that there is a positive association between aid to the poor and investment in children via increasing the income of parents or more likely "parent". But welfare payments make it possible for single mothers to live alone. This change in the character of the family unit is likely to reduce the investment in children. In addition, there is the anticipated increased income of the next generation via welfare if they do not get educated. I would suggest that these latter effects outweigh the income effect of welfare on parents.

Many of these unintended consequences reduce economic growth. This effect is often mocked, especially by labor leaders. They sneer: "Trickledown economics". But significant effects on economic growth can have more than a trickle effect on the poor and middle-class. Mulligan (2013) argues that a substantial part of the increase in unemployment in the recent recession is attributable to the disincentive effects of the many increases in redistributive policies that occurred during the recession and shortly before it. In that analysis Mulligan just looked at the unintended consequences of redistributive policies. There would be even greater effects if one also considered the growth inhibiting effects of the vast increase in significant business regulations imposed during the recession years. Apart from the constraining effects of the regulatory requirements, the requirement of getting regulatory approval produces costs and time delays that slow growth.

Some sense of the impact of redistributive policies on economic growth is given by the expert panel assembled by the University of Chicago Booth School. This is a panel that includes both well-known liberal and conservative economists. They were asked in 2012, "Are economists advice on tax policy influenced by their views on growth versus redistribution?" 75 percent answered "Yes." 25 percent did not answer and 0 percent answered "No" (Chicago, 2012).

These results reflect the dominant view among economists that there is a trade-off between growth and redistribution, though that view is not unanimously shared, for example Stiglitz, 2015. If this dominant assessment is correct, certain important conclusions follow. First, an unintended consequence of redistribution is less growth. Second, that effect is great enough for some economists to be against the redistributive tax policy offered by others. Third, some economists knowing of this trade-off still opt for a redistributive tax policy.

Economists have often phrased this trade-off as the efficiency-equity trade-off. In Fuchs et al.(1998) expert Labor Economists were at the mean slightly in favor of more equity and expert Public Economists were slightly in favor of more efficiency, but they all recognized the existence of that trade-off.

One form of aid to the needy, aid to the unemployed, has another deleterious impact. Unemployment has a serious psychological cost for most people. There is a pride associated with being a bread winner, work provides a focus to existence, a focus that makes evolutionary sense. Man has always worked, and most people would be lost without that focus. Brooks (2013) finds 80% of U.S. workers get some satisfaction out of their jobs. Any policy that reduces the incentive to work will reduce that psychological return from work.

Another source of inefficiency from aid to the needy in our society is that most of that aid is delivered through government agencies of one sort or another. Voters have little information about the details of government administration. Special interests and general problems with an uncontrolled bureaucracy are well-known features of government operations. Not only is aid to the poor subjected to these difficulties, but it makes all other government operations worse by increasing the size of government. All of the problems of government are made worse the larger governmental size. In part that is because voters' limited information has more deleterious consequences, the greater the information requirements for proper supervision of governmental activities.

One of the most serious consequences of an enlarged government is the increase in bureaucratic decision-making. The number of decisions Congress can make is limited so an increase in the required number of decisions increases the number of decisions Congress delegates to bureaucrats. That affects the character of democracies. Bureaucrats are not a random sample of the general population. They are not just experts, but they are advocates. For example, people who choose to work for the Environmental Protection Agency tend to be environmentalists. Climatologists tend to believe in using resources to achieve their goals. It is not simply that self-interested bureaucrats have an interest in expanding their bureaus. They tend to really believe that such expansion is in the common good far more than the electorate in general. Those beliefs are not based on their expertise. Rather it is the beliefs that help generate the motivations to acquire the expertise in the first place.

Naïve altruism is not just confined to economic issues. It also manifests itself in issues of war and peace. Obviously, wars are costly, and so many argue that they should always be avoided at all costs. If all groups renounced force, there would be a net world gain. In their opposition to defense expenditures, naïve altruists often forget that some other groups have not renounced force. Those forceful groups have an obvious advantage over pacific groups. That by itself is contrary to the group interest of the pacifists, but it is combined with another impact of pacifism. Bellicose countries tend to have characteristics that most pacifists would regard as undesirable. Naziism or Sharia Law are not their preferred social arrangements

That the dominant determinants of voting positions are the political positions of one's friends and associates has an important consequence. Information about those political positions is both easy and important for the voter to acquire. In contrast, there is very little incentive to discover the consequences of the policy that a person and his friends advocate, and that is especially true when those consequences weaken the case for one's own political views. Indeed, there is an incentive not to discover consequences contrary to one's political position because one's own political position tends to be the position of one's friends. If discovery of such consequences leads one to change political positions, one risks the anger of one's friends.

Confirmation bias is particularly strong when the relevant information makes little difference to one's own life. It would be foolhardy to ignore consequences in market decisions, but that is not true of individual political decisions whose consequences have little impact on the individual decision maker because of the free-rider problem. Firms lay-off workers when demand for their products slacken. Otherwise their profits would be reduced. Countries often prohibit firms from doing so in spite of the long-run consequences of that policy – the reluctance of firms to hire workers in the first place.

The intended effects of a policy are not necessarily its direct effects. Take, for example, policies intended to reduce global warming by reducing CO_2. The goal of that policy is an indirect effect. Proponents of this policy have no trouble handling that indirectness. There is no confirmation bias discouraging them from learning about this indirect effect. This is another reason why the unintended consequences, at least the unintended consequences as far as the proponents of a policy are concerned, will tend to be unfavorable. If they were favorable, they would be included in the intended consequences.

Another Criticism of Liberals

Sowell (2009) presents one of the more influential criticisms of liberal voting behavior. He believes that what we regard as liberal altruistic voters behave the way they do because they have a vision of man's perfectability. Or, to put his analysis in our terms, liberals want to improve the world from its present state. That desire makes them altruists. What they don't recognize, however, is that their desire for a major transformation of our society fails to take account the virtues of present society that would be put at risk by their reforms. That makes them naïve.

Sowell's position stems in large part from the views of people like Burke or, more contemporaneously, Hayek (1988). Tradition produces better results than reforms that ignore that tradition. As discussed earlier, Hayek maintains that major beneficial institutions such as free markets and the family arose and subsisted through no reasoned planning, but occurred through a combination of self-interest and group survival. That lack of explicit voter approval makes trade and international trade in particular somewhat fragile. A large part of its support rests on traditional support because it exists. As a result, there is often popular resistance, particularly to international trade.

In terms of our analysis, traditionalism is one of the major sources of opposition to naïve altruism, but it is not the only one. Self-interest plays an important role as does a less naïve form of altruism.

Intentions vs. Consequences

Confirmation bias is not the only reason liberal altruists tend to ignore the unintended consequences of the policies they advocate. Some might believe that consequences are less important than intentions. The term "altruism" covers a variety of virtues. Altruism can focus on either the consequences of one's actions—that it helps other people. Alternatively, one can define "altruism" in terms of intentions—that one intends to help other people. In both cases altruism is usually associated with some self-sacrifice. However, when it comes to voting, as we have seen, there is virtually no self-sacrifice in an altruistic vote that has virtually no impact on policy because of the free-rider problem. But, for want of a better name, I will still call this "altruistic voting". The intentions are good even though there are no costs in having such intentions.

Actual behavior reflects both a concern with consequences and a concern with intentions The altruism associated with voting for the most part is an altruism toward strangers. Many people voting for the minimum wage do not know any of the workers getting less than the minimum wage, for example. Concern with the consequences of a policy toward others is the concern that a stranger would want from another. As far as strangers are concerned "the road to hell is paved with good intentions." All that a stranger gets from the altruism of others is determined by the consequences of the policies these others advocate whatever their intentions.

The story is quite different when one is dealing with altruism toward associates. Intentions are important in this case, in addition to consequences. That is the rationale for the exchange of gifts. When it comes to gifts, for example, it is, indeed, the thought that counts. A person can usually buy what he wants better than can another. That by itself would generate only gifts of cash. But the non-cash gift also signals an empathy toward one felt by another more than a cash gift. If successful, such a gift shows an insight into a person's preferences not shown by a simple cash gift. But even when the gift is not a winner, it shows that the gift giver has favorable intentions toward the gift receiver.

To say that it is "intentions" rather than "consequences" that is crucial in gift-giving is missing some of the point. The statement is correct as far as looking at the immediate impact of the gift-giving is concerned. But that is because the intentions appropriately forecast long run consequences. The intentions are associated with a continuation of relationships between the parties involved in the gift exchange. Those relationships involve both reciprocity in helping behavior between the two and a construction of satisfying emotional bonds.

Neither of those long run consequences of intentions holds in the case of altruism between strangers, strangers both before and after the altruistic display. However, voters can use a display of intentions as a forecast of consequences. There is evidence that intentions make a difference in political choice in addition to consequences. A standard question asked in surveys of voters political attitudes is whether a candidate cares about people like the respondent. These polls do not ask whether a candidate's policies will be favorable toward people like the respondents. These are not the same questions because one focuses on intentions—empathy—and the other on consequences. But these are similar questions to voters who view stated intentions as a good predictor of consequences. The empathy polls always show a substantial advantage of Democratic candidates. For example, Exit Polls in 2012 showed that among voters who regarded Presidential empathy as important 81% voted for Obama, while only 12% voted for Romney (Fox News,2012). It is far easier to display empathy by advocating more redistribution than opposing that redistribution on the grounds that its indirect effects are deleterious. It is easier to ascribe self-interest motives to such opposition.

Intentions would be a useful signal of consequences in a zero-sum economy, where gains to one person must come as a comparable loss to others. The statistical fact that Republicans are the party of the rich means in that scenario that they would be less helpful to others. That Romney was rich fortified the signaling stereotype of the less than empathetic character of Republicans. The richness of a Democrat would have less negative connotations if that Democrat were advocating heavier taxes on the rich. Democrats necessarily win the political game in a zero-sum world, and it is not surprising that "fairness" is their mantra with its emphasis on "gender, race, and class." That theme is even made more persuasive when the Democrats have candidates belonging to one of the "oppressed" on the premise that a woman is more likely to understand the problems of women etc.

This form of identity politics has had impacts well beyond the current political scene in the United States. It doomed colonialism. The end of British rule, for example, often resulted in the exchange of an African dictator for a British one. This was probably a popular exchange even though its consequences were often devastating. The African ruler was assumed more empathetic toward his fellow Blacks than any white man would be. It is easy to understand how this attitude developed. Conquered groups have often been wiped out by conquerors, and genocide is still a real possibility in many regions of the world. Identity politics is a natural extension of xenophobia. It is an extension that works most effectively among those groups that have some basis for feeling exploited. In particular, lower income groups such as Blacks and women play the identity game more than others. There are no "White man" ethnic studies.

There is another reason why voter intentions play a role apart from consequences. Because of the free-rider problem, no voter has a substantial impact on policy. They might as well ignore the consequences that they do not affect. Being good is good enough.

This belief in the power of intentions is inconsistent with Adam Smith's invisible hand – that greedy business's help the poor not because they intend to but because competitive pressures make them do so. These businessmen need not be very empathetic, but empathy is not a prerequisite for their performing a vital social service. That invisible hand is also inconsistent with the notion of a zero-sum economy. Our previous discussion of deadweight losses is a discussion about costs to the economy of redistribution, costs that are inconsistent with a zero-sum economy.

Of course conservative politicians are not businessmen. Their central interest, just like the interest of liberal politicians, is getting elected or reelected. They can also have other intentions which help govern their choice of the party under whose banner they fly. Republican politicians tend to be pro-free market both in their rhetoric and their actions if elected. It is the interest of businessmen that they represent, interests which are selfish but beneficial to the economy, if many economists are correct.

A possible paradox is thereby produced where intentions and consequences move in opposite directions. Government policies produced by naïve altruists with the best of intentions can lead to problematic consequences because unintended consequences are ignored. In contrast, to the extent that the invisible hand operates, unfettered selfish business decisions can lead to favorable consequences. This comparison of government policies and business decisions ignores another important feature of government. Government officials are not simply naïve altruists. They are also self-interested, which produces another set of unfortunate consequences of government action. The self-interest of business is seriously constrained by competitive pressure. If a business does not supply what consumers want, some other firm will do so. There are rarely other firms competing with government, so government officials are not constrained by competition.

In the voting case, if intentions were simply a forecaster of consequences, then known actual consequences would trump intentions when those intentions did not yield favorable consequences. And I believe that is at least partially the case, as is suggested by the evidence of Chapter 4. But there can be some built in characteristics, such as xenophobia, that still make voters respond favorably to declared intentions. Furthermore, confirmation bias would operate in this case just as in the case of unintended consequences. A favorable response to declared intentions would make a voter reluctant to examine consequences that would run counter to that initial response.

CHAPTER 3

COLLEGES: THE HEARTLAND OF NAÏVE ALTRUISM

The Intellectual Class

That university teachers are dominantly liberal is well known. That that fact is important might be somewhat less obvious. Most of the other people who have a more than average influence on public opinion have gone to universities and they have been influenced by their college experience. Gross and Simmons (2007) find that students become more liberal politically between their freshman and senior years. Nelson and Greene (2003) show that the college educated are most liberal on the issues that college teachers are most liberal. Another example, the political orientation of newspapers was quite different in the old days when journalists did not go to college compared to their current orientation. There has been much talk about the limousine liberals. The most obvious way they got that way is through their college experience and their association with their fellow college graduates.

Not only are college teachers liberal. They are liberal by huge majorities. According to Gross and Simmons (2007) 78% of college teachers who supported major parties were Democrats around 2004. That percent for the population in 2004 was 53, and, of course, Democrats are more liberal than Republicans. The difference is easily significant at the 1% level.

This dominance of liberals in college teaching holds especially for most of the disciplines which deal with public policy. Gross and Simmons (2007) examine party affiliation for the twenty major disciplines in 2004. Of those disciplines English and the non-economic social sciences stand out in two characteristics – the smallest percentage of Republicans and the largest percentage of Democrats. These two percentages are not mirror images of one another, since there are is a substantial percentage of Independents. (They classify Independent Leaning Democratic, Independent, and Independent Leaning Republican as Independents). Of the five fields that can be so characterized (English, Psychology, Political Science, Sociology, and History) the lowest percent of Republicans was in English (2 percent) and the highest percent of Democrats was in History (79 percent).

This overwhelming liberalism in these disciplines was not always the case. There is, indeed, evidence that college curricula have changed over time, requiring more and more courses in multiculturalism, for example. Rothman et al. (2005) summarize their examination of the evidence. "Among college teachers in the humanities and the non-economic social sciences conservatives went from being merely underrepresented in the decades after World War II to being nearly extinct in the 1990's."

Kimball (2008) has an explanation for this sea change – a cultural revolution in the 1960's that occurred in the United States and Western Europe. The 1960's were the age of the Beats and other related radical groups. But, of course, this explanation requires an explanation. The most obvious relevant technological developments were the widespread use of birth control pills and the reduction of home work that freed more women to enter the labor force. Sex could be separated from reproduction. Under those circumstances the old sexual mores seemed less relevant to many, in particular to women, who would bear most of the brunt of unwanted pregnancies. It is significant that one of the intellectual movements that blossomed during the sixties was feminism. Gross (2013) finds that most of the increased liberalism in the professorate since the sixties occurred among women professors, 63% of whom describe themselves as feminists. This questioning of sexual traditions led to a questioning of traditions in general. Traditions do seem to come in a bundle. If a person finds tradition a less satisfactory basis for behavior in one area, he is less likely to find it a satisfactory answer in other areas. Social conservatives are more likely to be economic conservatives than others. In support of that proposition Jost et al. (2003) found that those more willing to experiment and have new experiences tended to be political liberals. I maintain with evidence that what people tended to substitute for tradition was naïve altruism.

The outsized liberalism of college professors has had a substantial influence on the political position of others. College professors have a reputation as knowledgeable and they have a captive audience on which to proselytize. That liberal influence is all the greater because the big liberals among university teachers are in fields where policy is talked about the most. (The effect of a liberal physicist on students' political positions is probably minimal.) Gross (2013) tries to minimize the liberalization of the faculty by focusing on the whole faculty rather than the ones that count in terms of the transmission of political preferences. As a result, college students become more liberal through the college experience (Gross and Simmons (2007)). (The other obvious reason is being away from home.) We would expect this effect to be strongest among the students who attend the more prestigious universities, since that is where the liberalism among college faculties is the strongest. Community colleges –included in the Gross and Simmons (2007) sample- and non- liberal arts B.A. granting colleges have the most conservative faculty. 37 percent of community college faculty and 39 percent of non-liberal arts B.A. granting schools are liberals compared to 57 percent of Elite Phd. granting schools and 61 percent of the liberal arts BA granting schools (Gross and Simmons (2007)). This should have a significant liberalizing effect on future leaders who tend to attend these more prestigious schools. Only 3 percent of social scientists and 6 percent of those in the humanities strongly agree that their political views should be kept out of the classroom. (The more relevant question is whether the opposite views from their own should be included in the classroom, but Gross and Simmons (2007) does not ask that question.)

Why are university faculty so liberal and why is that phenomenon strongest in the humanities and the non-economics social sciences? I believe the reason is simple. There is a good reason why social scientists should be more altruistic as far as policy is concerned. One of the interest areas of the social sciences and philosophy" is what generates a good society, the object of altruism. Altruism is part of their job description. They are paid to be altruists. This sounds like an oxymoron, but both their being paid and their belief that they are being altruistic have real consequences.

Of course, social scientists are not being fully altruistic even in the sense that I use the word. To some extent the social scientists could be interested in helping social scientists. They would tend to support more expenditures for colleges, but that is a minor part of the liberal agenda. Even their special enthusiasm for greater education expenditures could be attributable to selection bias. One of the reasons they selected a college career could have been their disinterested belief in the importance of colleges.

The story is somewhat different for the non-philosophic humanities. Society has not assigned them the task of determining what constitutes the good society. But they have taken up that task on their own. In the past they focused more on aesthetics. But poverty and greed were often the focus of the literature they studied. The nature of literature is to put its readers in the place of others. Empathy is a central component of altruism. A novelist is not tasked with the job of determining the unintended consequences of social policy on two counts. He is, for the most part, dealing with interpersonal relationship where, as we have seen, intentions are often more important than immediate consequences. Secondly, even when he deals with social policy, the novelist has no reason to go beyond the obvious social concerns that motivate naïve altruism.

The English case is instructive. Why should a discipline focused on aesthetics be in the forefront of liberal political preference? The answer is that aesthetics is no longer the central focus of English Departments. Aesthetics seemed largely irrelevant in the struggle against conservatives, a struggle made popular among intellectuals by the Cultural Revolution of the 1960's. In consequence, English Departments reinvented themselves. Political preferences affected much more than how English professors voted. It affected what they did. The political preference came first, and the research agenda followed. This is not just a proposition asserted by conservatives. Liberal humanists declare as much. Their rationale is that politics is everywhere and, hence, unavoidable (Kimball, 2008). Part of the reason so much reinvention occurred in English Departments is because there never was a central discipline that held the field together. This allowed a kind of flexibility not possible in many other fields. One would not expect a politically correct physics to develop for example. Biology, though, has produced certain tendencies in that direction. There have been attempts to conform to political ideology around evolutionary issues: Lysenko's inheritance of acquired characteristics or Creationism, but those attempts barely got off the ground because they ran counter to the evidence. In contrast, English is not evidence based.

Another reason English Professors are in the forefront of political liberalism is that the central focus of their studies is fiction. Psychologists have found that fiction makes the reader more empathetic. Reading non-fiction does not (Mar, et al. 2009). That would tend to make English Professors more politically altruistic, transferring results from the interpersonal relationships on which fiction focuses to the political world.

One of the current sub-fields in English Departments is Cultural Studies. One of its premises is that capitalists use culture to control the masses. Cultural Studies' objective is to connect the study of culture to a larger progressive political project (Wikipedia, 2014). Notice, the object of the research is not to question whether capitalism brainwashes the masses through culture to support capitalism. They assume that impact and their job is to demonstrate its assorted manifestations.

What makes that endeavor somewhat amusing is that current culture is so obviously liberal in its orientation. Not only are universities that way but Hollywood, writers, and musicians are all predominantly liberal not only in their politics but in the works they produce. But a little reality is not enough to stop the burgeoning of Cultural Studies. That burgeoning is fostered in part by the intellectual fog of its proponents. For example, look at the physicist Alan Sokal's parody of Cultural Studies, a parody in which Sokal peppered his paper with what he regarded as nonsense phrases. However, it was published as the real thing by Social Texts, a Cultural Studies journal.

As detailed by Kimball (2008) many of the most prestigious humanity professors make no pretense that their liberalism is due to any careful examination of the evidence. They often deny that there is any way to be objective in general, and, therefore, see no need that they should be. Indeed, objectivity is often viewed as intrinsically reactionary, and,hence, evidence of a bad mindset of those who wish to pursue it. In Gross's interviews with English professors all denied the possibility of objective knowledge. Under those circumstances they clearly make no claim that their political position is knowledge based.

Sociologists are not so overwhelmingly deniers of objective knowledge as English professors, though many belong in the denier camp (Gross, 2013). One would suspect that the deniers would be the most politically active. Sociology has as one of its aims to understand and reduce social inequality, according to the liberal Gross (2013). "Concerns about inequality, oppression, social justice diversity, recognition, and tolerance loom large" in sociology courses. As examples Gross (2013) lists some of the courses taught in the sociology graduate program at Wisconsin: "Feminism and Sociological Theory", "Intercultural Dialogues," "Environmental Stewardship and Social Justice", and "Class, State and Ideology: An Introduction to Marxist Sociology". Sex and gender studies is the "second largest group in the American Sociological Association. Problems generated by forced income equalization tend to be short changed in such an intellectual environment.

In this context it is somewhat amusing to hear liberals label conservatives as anti-intellectual or anti-science if both are defined in terms focusing on the search for truth. The attitude of most in the humanities and many in the non-economic social sciences can properly be called anti-intellectual intellectualism. It is an attitude that hardly justifies their reasons for being if one does not share their politics. "Why should a conservative subsidize these openly declared political beings?" many do say.

The anti-intellectual label on conservatives has some merit when some social conservatives deny evolution. But that denial has minimal consequences on political agendas, mainly on whether alternative theories to evolution should be taught. Contrast that with the feminist denial of many biological differences between genders, a denial that has more serious political consequences. Perhaps the most celebrated case was the forced resignation of the liberal Larry Summers as President of Harvard. In 2006 he said that there might be different levels of aptitude for science between men and women at the highest cognitive level. The Harvard faculty found even the suggestion that there might be such gender differences too much. It certainly brings into question that faculty's commitment to the dispassionate search for truth when that truth might be inconsistent with its political preferences.

There have been claims that liberals are more tolerant of political differences than conservatives, but that evidence is all about attitudes toward people who have views more similar to the views of liberals than conservatives, for example, attitudes toward Communists (Liberals share with Communists some skepticism about the efficacy of free-markets.) The current behavior of colleges toward those with conservative ideas certainly does not suggest that liberals have a high tolerance threshold.

Economists vs. the Humanities and Other Social Scientists

As discussed earlier, there are serious unintended consequences of most government programs to help the needy. Some people, in particular many economists, believe that these consequences are serious enough that these government programs should be reduced. Many of these government program skeptics share with the naïve altruists an interest in the good society. They are both altruists, though they come up with drastically different policy views. Clearly, these skeptics do not dominate the university teacher ranks.

My claim is that university teachers in the humanities and in the non-economic social sciences are for the most part naïve altruists. They do not take into account the unintended consequences of their altruism. For some evidence of that proposition look at the considerable literature in political science devoted to the broader issue of the impacts of lack of voter information in the political process. In general, failure to mention something in an article is not an indicator that the author is unaware of that something. One would not expect an article about nuclear physics to mention the unintended consequences of government policy because those consequences are irrelevant to the topic discussed. I maintain, however, that lack of information about unintended consequences is one of the most important information deficiencies of voters. Yet as noted in my previous discussion about the political science discussions of voter information, those discussions do not mention information about unintended consequences. Those political scientists are either unaware of those unintended consequences are think them unimportant.

Gross and Simmons (2007) provide additional evidence. Look at the percentage Democrats among those who expressed a party preference and whose disciplines were specified by Gross and Simmons (2007). That percentage was 55 for Economists; 90 for Sociologists; 89 for Political Scientists; 96 for English; 92 for Psychology; 95 for History.[2]

These numbers have a number of important properties. First, there is a huge difference between party preferences for Economists and any of the other humanities and social sciences that Gross and Simmons (2007) specify. Klein (2007) also finds a substantial difference. The party preferences of economists are approximately the same as that for the general population. The party support of all of the other disciplines are all approximately the same as each other at an extremely high level of support for Democrats. My explanation for all of these results centers on economists' concern with the unintended consequences of naïve altruism, a concern that the other disciplines do not share.

There is a reason why one would expect economists to be more Democratic than the general population. They do a lot more associating with their university colleagues than does the general population. With whom one associates helps determine political positions. In fact, economists are slightly more Democratic than the general population, but by only a trivial amount. That approximate equality in party support suggests that the association effect is balanced by some other factor. The most obvious other factor is that economists are not only more concerned with unintended consequences than their university colleagues, but are more concerned about them than the general population.

Are Unintended Consequences Consequences?

Gross (2013) offers another explanation of the relative conservatism of economists from the view point of the other social sciences. They complain that economists use rational behavior models when everybody knows that much behavior is irrational. That complaint is shared by many economists who are Behavioral Economists. They cite many features of human behavior that are inconsistent with simple rational behavior models. For example, the dual behavior of many alcoholics whose preferences are very different when they are off or on the wagon. Indeed, this attitude of some economists provides a rationale for similar criticism of standard economics by other academics. For example, the biologist, Wilson, believes he is justified in his criticism of standard economics because his criticism is consistent with that of some economists (Wilson, 2015). The point, I guess, is that if one has a position that requires bolstering by the views of an economist, one can always find an economist with those views. Confirmation bias at work.

But the fact that there is more to behavior than encompassed by most economic models does not prevent these models from being exceedingly useful. Economists have been remarkably successful in both explaining and predicting behavior with their rational behavior model. Indeed, most of the predictions of microeconomics arise from a further simplification –that markets are competitive. We know that in many markets that is not true in the strictest sense, and that fact has been emphasized by many economists in justifying liberal policies, for example Stiglitz (2015). But the crucial empirical implications of the competitive model work nonetheless.: incentives matter, and the lower the real price, the greater the quantity demanded and the less the quantity supplied. Those predictions work in spite of assorted noises created by a variety of processes. That noise would reduce the magnitude of the effects predicted by economic models if those models predicted magnitudes. But the models only predict directional effects. The magnitudes have to be determined by empirical work, and that work for the most part has shown substantial effects.

There is another process that increases the predictive power of economic models. Those businesses that profit maximize are more likely to survive than those that do not. Bankruptcies are a common phenomenon in the United States. Avoiding bankruptcies requires firms to at least break even. That is easier to do if firms maximize profits, which usually requires them to use less of a resource whose price has risen and to reduce output in response to an imposed reduction in price.

Survival is a less constraining consideration as far as consumers and workers are concerned in the United States. Few die because they make foolishly irrational decisions in the market. Still some sensible decision-making is built into their genes. There was a time when irrational behavior would have serious survival consequences. In consequence, as a matter of fact, migrants tend to move where they can get higher real income, and people do respond to lower prices whether they are businessmen or not.

It is those two implications that are at the heart of the unintended consequences of the liberal agenda. For example price controls create shortages because at the lower price demanders want more and suppliers supply less, for example, the long lines at gas stations whenever governments impose maximum prices on gasoline. It is no wonder that the rest of the social sciences fail to consider unintended consequences when they reject the foundations on which those claims are made. The denial of incentive effects on the grounds of behavioral economics displays only a superficial knowledge of economics. A common feature of this denial is to only quote the few studies that support that denial, and to ignore the rest: confirmation bias operating full throttle.

Often the denial of unintended consequences produces a kind of schizophrenia. Almost everybody recognizes supply and demand in ordinary discourse. Who would deny that a big increase in the supply of oil drives oil prices down? But the same analysis is not accepted by many when it is involved in examining the consequences of government policy.

But because of "irrational behavior" consumers can make mistakes, which can provide some rationale for some of the kind of market interferences that liberals like. However, the policies thus affected are a very small part of the liberal agenda. Banning tobacco is not a core issue separating liberals from conservatives.

However, the incompleteness of economists' rational behavior models has had an influence on some economists similar to the influence that it has had on the rest of social science. Some Behavioral Economists reject the standard rational behavior model as a useful tool. In addition, most Macroeconomists do not focus on the unintended consequences that are a feature of economists' rational behavior model. Indeed, confirmation bias affects Keynesian economists in much the same way that it affects the non-economic social scientists. Government expenditures, in their view, are an effective anti-recession tool. They would prefer to ignore the fact that those expenditures are not a perfect substitute for private market expenditures and have consequences on that market place different than their mechanical multiplier effect.

Even some micro-economists question the predictive power of standard economics, though their objections are concentrated on the competitive model rather than the assumption of rational behavior. Mulligan (2014) found that 70 percent of Intermediate Microeconomic texts are devoted to imperfect competition rather than perfect competition. With imperfect competition models it is possible that the simple implications of perfect competition would not hold. For example, if some process increases prices but it somehow makes the firm's demand curve look more like the competitive demand curve, it could increase the quantity that a firm would supply. But it might not. This is characteristic of imperfectly competitive models. They tend to produce ambiguous results unless one knows far more than the existence of imperfect competition, a knowledge rarely possessed. In spite of the greater emphasis on imperfect competition in economic theory classes, most of the predictive power of economics is generated by simple competitive models. But the emphasis on imperfect competition has reduced many economists faith in those models.

However imperfectly related to the competitive ideal, private market expenditures are much more closely related to the competitive ideal than government expenditures, in particular the unintended consequences of those expenditures. The virtues of that fact are detailed below. Governments are under no competitive pressure to get it right. Furthermore, governments frequently act as if they were dealing with other people's money, reducing their incentives to use that money efficiently compared with the personal incentives of bureaucrats to benefit themselves and their pet causes.

There is another objection to the standard way economist examine the unintended consequences of many policy proposals, an objection that is more general than the complaints of the Behavioral Economists. The standard economic tool to examine these consequences is called "deadweight loss". If there were perfectly competitive product and resource markets, no externalities, and demanders' wants perfectly reflected demanders' benefits, there would be no deadweight loss. Deadweight loss is the amount of money people would be willing to pay to move from the quantity of the product produced to the ideal amount.

The ideal competitive determination of the quantity of a product produced is that optimal amount. At the intersection of the demand and supply curves the marginal benefits of the product would just equal the marginal social cost of its production. Producing more would increase costs more than it increased benefits. Producing less would reduce benefits more than it reduced costs. Either of those latter scenarios produces deadweight loss.

Those who try to measure the cost of the unintended consequences of policy, do so by assuming that in the absence of these unintended consequences an ideal competitive equilibrium would prevail. But even in the absence of government intervention, the actual economy is not the same as the competitive ideal. That fact has been emphasized by many economists persuaded by the arguments of Lipsey and Lancaster in their much quoted "General Theory of the Second Best" (1968). They assert, "It is not true that when more of the (*ideal competitive*) conditions are fulfilled, (*that state*) is necessarily or even likely to be superior to a situation in which fewer are fulfilled." In other words, further interferences with market solutions do not necessarily move one further from the competitive ideal when that ideal has not been achieved in the first place.

They are right in terms of necessity. An interference can move one toward the competitive ideal. But they are wrong in terms of likelihood at least as far as unintended consequences are concerned. The best analogy of this process is shuffling a deck of cards. Think of the extant deviation from the competitive model as one shuffle of the deck otherwise in some perfect order. Think of the unintended consequences of a government action as another shuffle. The expected result is that second shuffle together with the first shuffle causes the deck to be arranged further from the original perfect order than just the first shuffle alone, but there is some small probability that the second shuffle brings the deck closer to that perfect order. I look at this problem in more detail in the Appendix.

This analogy assumes that the unintended consequences were random interferences with markets. It turns out, however, that most of the unintended consequences of naïve altruism are not random interferences with the market. They systematically make things worse. As already recounted, many of those interferences are motivated by redistributive incentives. They almost always interfere with the operation of a largely competitive labor market. Even when the market is less competitive because of the union effect, government interferences tend to be pro-union. Then, there is the neglect of costs of government policy by decision makers. We discuss that issue more thoroughly later. That understates the cost of policies in the appropriate but largely unused cost-benefit analysis.

A substantial number of economists have abandoned rational behavior models when it comes to examining the consequences of government policy. However, Gross is right in asserting that economists can be distinguished from other social scientists by the extend they use such models only because so few of the latter examine the unintended consequences of government policy in terms of those models.

This agreement between Gross and myself lends credence to the proposition that rational behavior models distinguish economists from the other social sciences. Gross has a quite different policy perspective than I do, so this proposition does not depend upon policy preferences. Gross seems to imply that this rational perspective of economists is a failing.

I have tried to show why economists are right in looking at unintended consequences with those models. So these unintended consequences are real, and those who ignore them can justifiably be called naïve.

There is a more general proposition with respect to government-induced social change. The previous social arrangements occurred as a result of a long evolutionary process. These arrangements started either by group choice or some other process. Whatever the initial thrust, they have managed to survive. Defining "better off" in terms of social survival, the unintended consequences of changing these arrangements will be unfavorable. But we can have less confidence in this more general argument than in the previous discussion of the virtues of the free market. In that discussion we can specify exactly what is unfavorable about the unintended consequences. Without that specification, the general conservative argument has less force. Besides social survival is somewhat different than the welfare criterion we later propose , though they are somewhat related.

However, one of the unintended consequences of the welfare program seems to be an example of the operation of this more general proposition. There is survival value to a society in having high quality children. We would, therefore, expect social arrangements to evolve that further that goal. In a culture where the nuclear families play an important role in child rearing, single motherhood is antithetical to that goal and its increase is an unintended consequence of the welfare program. The desirability of high-quality children goes far beyond a simple evolutionary criterion. It is consistent with the value criterion we later develop.

Hayek (1988) has a related argument for the problems associated with altruism. The great advantage of self-interest is that one is likely to know the self-interested consequences of one's actions, but the effects on other people are only partially known even to a person who is trying to be altruistic. Even if an altruist knew those effects, an altruist would be hard put to justify the particular weights he should give the individual people whose well-being he is trying to maximize. How much more weight should the altruist give to the well-being of Blacks or women than to that of others, for example? That is not a problem when one focuses simply on one's own self-interest.

A related complaint against economists, according to Gross, is that economists do not focus on redistributional issues enough. Relative to the other social sciences and the humanities that observation is correct. Economists' approach to the world cannot be simply summarized as "race, class, and gender." However, economists do concern themselves with income distribution both in positive and normative terms. Economists are likely to be utilitarians. Most utilitarian economists believe in the diminishing marginal utility of money, that at the margin the poor get greater utility per dollar than do the rich. Such a belief does not make one a conservative. For example, a majority of economists are in favor of the minimum wage. The only justification for such support is redistributional. Klein and Stern (2007) found that economists believed in redistribution to the poor. Fuchs et al. (1998)' survey of expert Labor and Public Economists got similar results.

Though economists do deal with redistribution, it is possible that they don't deal with it enough. It is possible that if they knew more, they would focus more of their attention on "race, class, and gender", the favorite triplet of the rest of the social sciences. But why should that be the case? There is a much more persuasive argument that the other social sciences focus on these issues in a very distorted way generated by another manifestation of confirmation bias. Not only do naïve altruists ignore unintended consequences, but they try to downplay anything which would minimize the grievances they have with the operation of free markets. If, for example, it is genetic differences that make more men go into science than women, that would be a state of the world hardly the fault of capitalism.

One of the solutions naïve altruists have offered for gender inequality in pay is "comparable worth"—a proposed mandate that all occupations with the same level of education be paid the same. Art historians with a Phd. should be paid the same as nuclear physicists with a Phd. That is a way to equalize the gender pay differences associated with occupational choice. That would also produce the devastating unintended consequences produced by price controls, unintended consequences that are ignored by the advocates of "comparable worth".

The market pays nuclear physicists more than art historians because at the margin nuclear physicists produce more than art historians as the worth of products are evaluated by the market. Even if one objected to this system of determining the value of products, using comparable worth would produce unpleasant consequences unless one substituted government evaluation of product worth for the market's evaluation, a proposal with devastating consequences of its own. At nuclear physicists salaries unemployment of art historians would be even more rampant than it is now.

Similarly, confirmation bias makes naïve altruists reluctant to discuss the many pathologies associated with the plight of inner city blacks: high crime and minimal education. Or if they do discuss these issues, they find a single culprit – poverty, poverty produced one way or another by capitalism or other evils created by the white majority. The idea is to make the grievances associated with "race, class, or gender" appear to be as great as possible, a way of fortifying the current focus of naïve altruism. .

Nor are economists unconcerned with the environment, the other big issue separating liberals and conservatives. There is a branch of economics called "Environmental Economics." Indeed, Klein and Stern, 2007, found that economists in general were supporters of environmental regulation. For environmental issues economists, for the most part, depend upon cost-benefit analysis. But this analysis could only reject any liberal environmental policy if that analysis rightly included the costs that are unintended consequences of those policies.

There is one more explanation for economist's peculiar behavior. "They are crass; they are materialists," some might charge. But expenditures on culture use up resources just like any other expenditure. Economists do tend to take the preferences of people as givens. "If they want to spend more on video games than on poetry, that's the way it is". People in the humanities might want to classify wants as higher and lower wants with their own wants obviously belonging to the former category. That difference might be important in the issue of government expenditures on the arts, but that is a relatively minor determinant of political positions.

Our own explanation for Economic Professors' distinctive behavior places them slightly out of our main framework of analysis. One of the functions of economics is to make policy recommendations. They, like their colleagues in the other social sciences, are expected to do so as altruists. But, in contrast to the others, most of them take unintended consequences into account in their policy evaluations. They are not naïve altruists. At the same time most of their associations outside of economics are with their fellow professors, most of whom are naïve altruists. So economists are neither fish nor fowl in the great divide between liberals and conservatives. In consequence, their behavior is a mixed bag not predictable from our analysis, though their behavior in relationship to their fellow professors is. But it is clear from the behavior of university professors in general that economists play only a minor role in the impact of colleges on political positions.

One possible reason for this phenomenon is that economists for the most part are not proselytizers. As detailed by Gross (2013), they are dedicated to the search for truth, according to their own assessments. This contrasts sharply with the admitted politicalization of the humanities and the rest of the social sciences. Microeconomists are usually loath to make policy recommendations, and the issues on which we focus are microeconomic issues. Currently, most economists are reluctant to make value judgments upon which policy depends. That non-political approach to its subject matter reduces the effect of confirmation bias. At the same time proselytizers on the whole are more successful at proselytizing than non-proselytizers.

There probably was a time when the political position of economists was much more important in colleges. That would require a considerable change in our view of the role of universities in determining political positions if we were dealing with that earlier period. The current relatively minor role that economists play in determining college opinion has an important consequence. Most altruists are naïve altruists.

The extremely high level of Democratic support among the humanities and the non-economic social sciences is some evidence that they do not examine unintended consequences. The unintended consequences examined previously are not trivial, the impediments to economic growth generated by redistribution for example. It is hard to imagine a discipline that seriously concerned itself with unintended consequences being so nearly unanimous in their Democratic support. That English leads the way makes that imaginary scenario even more imaginary.

We can get further insight into the processes that produce academia's liberal character by looking at academic boycotts of Israeli universities. In 2013 the American Studies Association started boycotting Israeli universities followed by the American Anthropological Association doing the same thing in 2015. Neither association pretended that these boycotts were produced by the expertise developed by their fields. Their rationale for their actions was that Israeli universities were parties to state policies that violated human rights. "Human rights" is a frequent component of the arguments of liberal altruism. One of the problems with this kind of altruism was discussed in the previous chapter. "Human rights" is such a vague concept that it can be used to rationalize virtually any action and, hence, is almost meaningless. There are just too many consequences of real world actions. Without some reasonable weighting of those consequences the "human rights" argument is empty. How important were the "human rights" of Israelis violated by Palestinian killings? Academia on the whole does not bother itself with such questions in its display of confirmation bias.

A real test of the neglect of the operation of confirmation bias by the humanities and the non-economic social sciences would require a detailed examination of their literature and their classrooms. We have some evidence in one case— political scientists that specialize in voter information. In my examination of their literature, none wrote about lack of information about the unintended consequences of many public policies. What I have found instead is an emphasis on informational deficiencies more likely to be possessed by conservatives, whether those deficiencies are very relevant to voter decisions are not. For example, Kuklinsky et al. (2000) asks "what percentage of the budget is spent on welfare" rather than "what percent of the budget is spent helping the poor" given that there are so many more anti-poverty programs than Aid to Dependent Children.

But even that question is less relevant to voters than the one on which Conard (2016)—decidedly not a political scientist— focuses. "How much do the poor unemployed receive per capita from governments relative to what they could make in the market?" His answer, $30,000 which is the same as the median income of Blacks and Hispanics. Both he and I would strongly suspect that that is relevant information to voters.

There is also relevant evidence about university bias in university administrations condemning "micro-aggressions" in the classroom. The explicit purpose of the anti "micro-aggressions " movement is to stop anything in the university that made students uncomfortable, particularly Afro-American students. But a troubling byproduct of that effort is to chill a lot of speech associated with conservatives. For example, the Office of the President at the University of California has condemned the following micro-aggressions among many of the same ilk: "I believe the most qualified person should get the job"; "Affirmative Action is racist", "America is the land of opportunity." The eminent legal scholar, Eugene Volokh believes that that condemnation means that uttering such phrases could get an untenured faculty member fired (Volokh, 2015). The academic personnel manual of the University of California states its approval of pro-liberal views, that research that highlights inequalities will be a factor in employment decisions.

The University of California is not alone. In a survey of 145 major universities, the Foundation for Individual Rights in Education found 133 placing restrictions on free speech with only 12 not doing so. Using less severe criteria, the Intercollegiate Institute found 46 universities decidedly uncomfortable for conservative and libertarian students, 63 with an uncomfortable environment, and only 15 with a comfortable environment (Heterodox Academy, 2016).

The public performance of universities suggests a strong intolerance for conservative views. If professors are intolerant of opposing views in their hiring decisions and in the life of the university in general, it would be unlikely that these same professors present these opposing ideas in their classroom and in their research. Their research in particular is likely to give short shrift to conservative ideas in part to be acceptable to their peers.

The most obvious cases of hiring discrimination are those of all the assorted ethnic and gender studies in universities. Each has its own point of view, that their particular group is oppressed. They insist that be the view of anybody they hire (Gross,2013) in spite of the fact that there are legitimate alternative views. (For example, some have stressed the breakdown of the black family and the income reducing choices voluntarily made by women.) That these studies are not involved in the dispassionate search for truth is obvious. In spite of this fact, these Studies have been accepted as legitimate by the rest of the university, at least sufficiently legitimate to be accepted without visible protest. At Bowdoin there are approximately the same number of students in these assorted Studies as in economics (Wood and Tascano, 2013). At Stanford in 1980 the faculty senate voted 39 to 4 to replace required courses in Western Civilization by a requirement that students take courses in "Culture, Ideas, and Values." That is an innocuous title until one examines the course content involved. Every course in the new requirement must include works by women, minorities or persons of color, and at least one work must address issues of race, gender, or class (Kimball, 2008) with the expectation that those issues be examined from a particular point of view. It is no wonder that universities in general do not object to the blatant biases of "Grievance Studies." That biased focus on "race, class, and gender" seems to be exactly what the university in general is pushing.

A 2014 report of the Young America's Foundation (The College Fix, 2014) found that over the three previous years the required reading program for freshman had no conservative books on the list of any of the many college programs they examined. There were, however, many books offering a liberal perspective on race, feminism, socialism, inequality, and wealth redistribution.

Much of the preceding evidence has been anecdotal, and there is a serious danger in using such evidence. The presenter of such evidence could advertently or inadvertently select evidence to bolster his case. However, the existence of assorted minority studies is a near universal in American colleges, and it is hard to conjure anecdotes that would contradict the previous anecdotes. "Race, gender, and class" are familiar categories in university pronouncements, and they are used to propose a similar treatment of these subjects that are associated with the explicitly propaganda nature of the studies devoted exclusively to these topics.

Other Explanations of Professors' Liberalism

There have been other explanations of the greater liberalism in colleges than elsewhere. But their partial operation does not invalidate the implications of one of our central propositions: the humanities and the non-economic social sciences do not take into account the unintended consequences of naïve altruism. Stigler (1982) used a self-interest explanation for the liberalism of college professors, that government is a source of grants and employment for them. But that explanation does not hold water with the possible exception of government's role in education. There is no positive relationship by discipline between recipients of grants and degree of liberalism. Furthermore, college teachers are far more liberal than other teachers and government employees in general in spite of the fact that a smaller percentage of the former are beholden to government (Nelson and Greene (2003)).

Gross (2013) provides another explanation of the liberalism of university professors: self-selection. Colleges have a reputation as bastions of liberalism. As a result liberals choose an academic career because they would be more comfortable among fellow liberals, and conservatives avoid university teaching careers because they think their political views would be impediments to advancement in an unfavorable environment. Gross's evidence is that most professors were liberals prior to starting graduate studies.

As Gross realizes, self-selection requires a reason that somebody should self-select. The most obvious reason is a prior reputation for liberalism in the professorate and that reputation has to come from somewhere. He believes that that reputation in the United States developed from special circumstances in the United States, in particular the affinity of professors to reform movements in the United States. But, the liberal professor is an international stereotype, not just a United States phenomenon, though there are only a few systematic studies of the political attitudes of professors outside the United States. Canada has the same pattern of political attitudes as the United States (Nakhaie and Brym 1999) –extreme liberalism among the humanities and the non-economic social sciences and relative conservatism among economists. That is a pattern shared by the Swedes as well (Berggren et al. 2010). Brooks (2014) also show that the political attitudes of professors in the United States are typical of the attitudes of professors in a multitude of countries, but the Brooks study has some highly questionable results. There is likely to be some general process common to most countries that produces professors' liberalism. The naïve altruism of college professors is such a process, a process that also works for Gross's particular explanation of the initial liberalism of professors in the United States.

At least part of the self-selection argument depends upon another selection process – professors selecting people with liberal views as their successors. Gross (2013) presents evidence both supportive and not of that hypothesis. He finds no tendency for professors to select liberals for their graduate programs. But he also finds that a substantial number of professors are willing to admit that neither Republicans nor fundamentalists would be welcome as colleagues, and that they scrutinized more carefully articles that have a different political perspective than their own. Both are natural human tendencies, and operate far more generally than just for those who explicitly declare their biases.

This selective process like self-selection requires a prior liberalism to determine that it is a liberalizing selection. Both processes multiply an initial liberal bias but cannot produce that bias. Both explanations are important however. They could explain how a dramatic event like the Cultural Revolution of the sixties could be perpetuated in less disruptive times. The sixties professors appointed their successors with their biases clearly in mind. In addition, the mild liberalism in the humanities made the radical takeover relatively easy. When a group not that much interested in politics confronts a group that is very interested, the very interested group tends to determine the political climate, especially if the relatively uninterested group mildly agrees with the interested group's inclinations. (I personally experienced this process in the Economics Department at the New School for Social Research in the sixties.)

More Predictions About College Teachers

We can make another prediction. College teachers in disciplines that do not discuss government policy should be more conservative than those in the humanities and the non-economics social scientists, since the kind of altruism that can affect political positions was less important in those former fields. Look at the percentage of Democrats among those having a major party preference in the three broad neutral disciplines listed by Gross and Simmons (2007): Computer Science and Engineering, 55; Health Sciences, 60; and the Sciences, 79. Two are significantly less than the percentages for each of the five non-economics social sciences and humanities, and all three are less than those five.

Equally interesting are the differences within these neutral disciplines. Both the percentages for Engineering and Health are significantly less than the percentages for the sciences. One would expect those in Engineering and Health to have far greater contact with the non-academic world than those in the sciences, since non-college jobs are so much more available in those sectors. That also is an explanation of why Gross finds that teachers in community colleges are more conservative than those in other institutions. Their faculty probably has more contact with people outside of their institution. That contact also generates greater conservatism among those who specialize in Business, who are also likely to have an economics background. The percentage supporting Democrats varied between 76 for those teaching Business Administration, 63 for those in Management Information to 41 for those in Accounting and 41 for those in Finance. The latter two are likely to have a larger background in economics than the former two.

The College Impact on Students

We expect college to make students more liberal, but there is another effect that operates in the opposite direction. College increases income which should make ex-college students more conservative. The standard way of controlling for this latter effect is to control for a person's family income. But that is an imperfect income control. A person's political position is not only a function of his own family income but the income of the people with which he associates. The greater a person's education the more likely he will associate with higher income people, thereby making him more conservative even when one controls for his own income.

Nelson and Greene (2003) provide evidence that permits one to disentangle these conflicting effects. It depends on the very mild liberalism of elementary and secondary teachers compared with the overwhelming liberalism of the college experience. Nelson and Greene (2003) have two variables, years of non-college education and years of college education which includes years beyond the BA. They also include a wide assortment of control variables like income, race, and gender. They also examined seventeen issues that divide liberals from conservatives such as attitudes toward increased welfare and environmental expenditures and Presidential votes.

There were six issues in which years of non-college education generated a significant conservative response and three in which there was a significant liberal response. But two of these latter responses are easily explained. The more years of non-college school the more favorable one is to increased education expenditures, a pretty obvious result. The other one is a non-economic issue, the more years of non-college school the more opposed to anti-abortion laws. The only economic issue for which years of non-college education produces a liberal response is environmental expenditures, which is less redistributive than the other issues. These results are consistent with the hypothesis that as far as elementary and secondary school education is concerned, an increase in years of school change political positions through the indirect effect of income even when one imperfectly controls for income.

The story is quite different for the effects of years of college education. There were twelve issues where that variable produced a significantly liberal response and only two that generated a conservative result. The liberalizing effect of the college educational experience clearly dominates the conservative income effect. It should be noted that these results were not simply a matter of the occupations of the college educated. The most obvious occupations such as educators college and otherwise, lawyers, and journalists were included as additional variables so did not directly affect the impact of years of college on political attitudes.

This liberalizing effect of the college experience is so great that even when one makes no attempt to control for income or race or anything, in 2008 and 2012 those whose college experience went beyond the BA were some of the strongest supporters of Obama. In 2012 a greater percentage of them voted for Obama than any other educational group. In 2008 their percentage was only topped by those with only a grade school education (Gallup, 2014).

There can be other processes producing this years of college effect. (We later talk about a cohort effect.) Further support for our explanation comes from comparing the political position of college seniors to college freshman. If college made one more liberal one would expect college seniors to be more liberal than college freshmen in the disciplines that advocated liberalism. Gross (2013) found this was the case for both the humanities and the social sciences but business majors became more conservative. These results for the social sciences understate the effect of liberal professors because economics is included in the social sciences and it is one of the most conservative disciplines.

There have been dramatic changes in the political positions of various professions that mirror the changes in the political positions of college teachers. Probably the most dramatic change has been the change in the legal profession. Nelson and Greene (2003) found that lawyers were more liberal than the general population controlling for a lot of other variables including years of college education. But this could be at least partially attributable to self-interest. Tort reform has been supported more by conservatives than liberals. But Nelson and Greene (2003) also report that among the issues that are not in the self-interest of lawyers the American Bar Association advocated sixteen liberal positions and one conservative positon. The American Bar Association in 1988 listed "sensitivity and "compassion" as some of the criteria for appropriate judicial appointments. (Silberman, 1990-91). Nelson and Greene (2003) also examined regression results from the General Social Survey 1972-1996 controlling for a multitude of other variables. They found that on 19 issues dividing conservatives and liberals, lawyers were significantly more liberal on four issues and not significantly conservative on any. One of those significantly liberal issues was presidential voting where the self-interest of lawyers was somewhat involved. This displays a rather moderate liberalism in contrast to the strong liberalism on display by the American Bar Association. That contrast is probably an example of a more general phenomenon. Organizations tend to be dominated by the more activist sub-set of their membership and the organizations tend to be more interested in the common self-interest of their membership than the membership itself. But even the political position of lawyers, and not their organization, is quite different than would accord with the old view of lawyers as a bastion of conservatism.

Bonica et al. (2015) get even stronger results for lawyerly liberalism. Using political contributions to candidates as a measure of degree of conservatism and a scale of 2 to -2, they find that attorneys average score is -.31 compared to an average score of contributor in generals as -.05. Furthermore, the liberalism of lawyers prevails in most practices that would not be affected by tort reform.

There is another Bonica result that suggests that this special liberalism of lawyers is due in part to the liberalism of their education. Of 48 legal practice areas the practice of law professor was the most liberal, beating out public defender by a little.

This liberalism of lawyers has obvious political consequences. The most common occupation from which legislators are drawn is "lawyer". And, obviously, the judiciary is even more dramatically occupied by lawyers. While voter preferences have a substantial effect on the character of their leaders, the pool from which those leaders are chosen is not irrelevant. For one thing, it effects the associates of the chosen, and association is an important determinant of political positions.

There is another group that we would expect to be influenced by its college experience. Journalists are dominantly Democratic, and the overwhelming character of this dominance is of relatively recent origin. Democratic party preferences were substantially greater than Republican party preferences. In 1971 35.5 % were Democrats and 25.7% were Republican. In 2013 the gap was much wider: 28.1% Democrats and only 7.1 % Republican (This Week, 2014).

The editorial endorsements of candidates is also interesting. Ansolabehere et al. 2006 show that in the 1940's and 1950's the endorsements substantially favored Republicans, while in the 1990's there was a 10% Democratic edge This result mirrors the journalists more liberal attitudes over time, but certainly does not correspond to journalists being liberals in the earlier years. Publishers play a role and their preferences would enter, especially into editorial endorsements. The Wall Street Journal is an example of a quite conservative editorial page that contrasts with news pages that cannot be so characterized. The higher income of publishers would on the whole make them more conservative, one would think. That thought was probably correct in the old days, but the dramatic change in the college effect has probably changed that income effect.

One would expect that this overwhelming liberal preference of journalists would generate some liberal bias in the media, though the media is in the business of pleasing its customers who have political attitudes preceding their encounters with the media. Groseclose and Milyo (2009) provide some evidence of this effect, though the research is not unanimous in that result. Gerber and Karlan (2009) have provided a convincing demonstration that the political position of a newspaper makes a substantial difference in the political position of its readers. They did so by randomly distributing the Washington Post and the Washington Examiner to readers and then tracking the resulting differences in political positions of those readers.

There is another group of the college educated that could have an impact on general political positions: elementary and secondary school teachers. Using General Social Statistics data from 1992-2004, The Audacious Epigone (2009) found that elementary school teachers voted Democratic in presidential elections slightly more than the general population—51% compared to 47%. There is no attempt to control for other variables, in particular gender. In consequence, that modest difference may not be attributable to their college experience. Using the same data source, but examining multiple issues and using multiple regressions, Nelson and Greene (2003) found that elementary and secondary school teachers were significantly liberal on three out of nineteen issues and not significantly conservative on any. Ignoring significance issue by issue, elementary and secondary school teachers had a liberal preference for thirteen issues and a conservative preference for four. Those results are significant at the 5% level. (These results do not include their significant support for greater educational expenditures for which they have a self-interested concern.) They were insignificantly liberal in their support for Democrats in general and in their support for Democratic presidential candidates.

The Nelson and Greene (2003) results understates the liberalism of elementary and secondary school teachers. They control for a multitude of variables, in particular, years of college education. In consequence, their results are for the degree of liberalism of non-college teachers beyond what is explained by average impact of years of college on liberalism. The same, of course, can be said for the Nelson and Greene (2003) results for lawyers and journalists. That suggests that the impact of college on the liberalism of lawyers and journalists is greater than its impact on non-college teachers, perhaps because the former are more likely to major in fields in college where liberalism is more pronounced.

This rather mild liberal position of elementary and secondary school teachers contrasts sharply with the very strong liberalism of teacher organizations. The 2013-2014 resolutions of the National Association of Educators is filled with liberal resolutions that have nothing to do with their self-interest as educators: resolutions to protect the whole gamut of human and civil rights as defined by liberals (NEA, 2014). We found a similar difference between the mild liberalism of attorneys and the ABA. Professional organizations seem to be captured by the most fervent. These probably have an outsized influence on the activities of the organization, in particular the crucial task of textbook selection.

I maintain that this cross-the-board liberalizing effect (in the political sense of that term) of the college experience is not attributable to the political and economic knowledge gained thereby. I regard it as more like an indoctrination effect. There is some evidence that the college experience does not create more political knowledge than others get simply by aging. Highton (2009) reports on the impact of college on two measures of political knowledge. The first measure is knowledge of a wide variety of political facts. The second is a measure of what he calls "political sophistication": knowledge that the Republican Party is more conservative than the Democratic Party and what that means. By both measures those who have been to college have more political knowledge than others, but not from the more aged of the latter.

Campaign Advertising

There are important consequences of the liberal bias of colleges, the media, and, to a lesser degree, elementary and secondary education. Democrats have been in the forefront of efforts to limit campaign contributions. Much of that effort has tried to exclude union contributions, easily explainable by unions being one of the major supporters of Democrats. But some of their efforts have focused on limiting campaign expenditures in general.

Some of the obvious forces at work do not explain this phenomenon. Limits on campaign contributions helps incumbents, but there are Republican incumbents as well as Democratic ones. Campaign spending can increase political interest. But Democrats have more to gain from greater interest, since the likelihood of their supporters voting is more sensitive to campaign interest than is the likelihood of Republican supporters voting. The greater proportion of Democrats voting in presidential election years than in other years is witness to that fact. Furthermore, there is no great Republican advantage in campaign expenditures. Often, Democrats outspend Republicans.

The most obvious explanation of Democratic support for campaign financing limits is that they have more to lose from increased information. Even with all the noise involved in campaign advertising, there is an information function. Campaign advertising is virtually the only information source in which Democrats and Republicans are on an even keel given the dominance of liberals in education and the media. An even distribution of information is more likely to benefit the party that has fewer information distributors than the party that has more. The more information the more of it will be repetitive and, hence, less influential.

CHAPTER 4

EVIDENCE: NAÏVE ALTRUISM AND INFORMATION

<u>Costs</u>

The government can improve the environment by directly paying for the improvement or requiring business to do so. In either case the proposed activity is costly. But costs are an unintended consequence of that activity, and hence to be downplayed by naïve altruists. They have to be aware that such costs exist. Their existence is too obvious for even the most naïve of altruists to deny. But they are capable of ignoring them nonetheless or maintaining that they are trivial compared to the great benefit of the particular policy.

Peterson (2014) provides an example of this process. In an Education Next poll respondent's support for increased educational expenditures fell from 66% to 44% when they were told the actual educational expenditures per student. Support fell to 26% when they were asked if they were in favor of taxes to fund those expenditures.

A Kaiser Foundation poll in 2009 found that 80% of Americans supported special funding for pre-existing medical conditions. Only 56% of those continued that support when they were told that that funding would raise their premiums (Instapundit, 2017).

It is little wonder that costs are not recognized in a lot of environmental regulation. The most dramatic example of this phenomenon is the EPA's interpretation of the Clean Air Act, that it does not have to take costs into consideration in regulating air pollution. Costs are also not considered in enforcing the Endangered Species Act. This downplaying of costs is not something environmentalists do surreptitiously. They proudly proclaim that position. For example, Farber (1999), a self-proclaimed moderate environmentalist, asserts that something beyond man's wellbeing should determine environmental policy. Such a position can be used to defend environmental expenditures no matter what they cost.

Sunstein (2015) provides additional evidence of the impact of information about unintended consequences on preferences, though that was not his intention. Sunstein reports on two polls in the United States from the late 1990's when the Kyoto Accord on climate change was up for debate. In one poll a strong majority agreed with the following statement: "Protecting the environment is so important that requirements and standards cannot be too high and continuing environmental improvement must be made regardless of cost." Roughly at the same time a majority said that they would oppose the Kyoto

Accords to constrain global warming if those accords would cost them personally fifty dollars a month or more.

What is remarkable is that respondents are able to respond to either poll. Crucial information is not specified in each. In the case of the first poll what is left out is how the costs of the Kyoto Accords are to be distributed among the citizenry. Of course, if one approves of the Kyoto Accords regardless of costs, then the distribution of costs would be irrelevant in determining one's approval. But it is hard to take seriously that hyperbole. No sensible person would really take that position. If the costs of Kyoto were high enough, everybody would starve in the process of implementing that accord. With the realization of trade-offs, the distribution of the costs of Kyoto would be relevant in determining support or opposition to Kyoto. The phrasing of the second poll also has its problem. In determining how much one is personally willing to pay to enforce Kyoto, one would want to know how much other people will be charged.

To determine the meaning of either poll one must guess at what respondents assumed in answering the poll. In the case of the second poll I believed respondents assumed that others would also be charged to pay for Kyoto. The reason for that belief is that that is the way government activities are financed. Nobody is asked to be the sole financier of any government action.

The respondents' response to the first poll is a little trickier to interpret because their actual response to "regardless of costs" makes no sense. It is obviously subject to a reducto ad absurdum. I believe that the first poll's respondents are ignoring costs in answering a question that specifically mentions costs. The "regardless of cost" phrase does not mean that respondents have examined costs, and have thereby decided that the benefits of global warming amelioration are so great that any actual costs in doing so are small in comparison. Rather, the "regardless of cost" phrase can be interpreted as "I need not examine costs." The big difference between the first and second poll is that the second uses the phrase "your personal costs" and the first does not. It is personal costs that others also pay that is relevant for determining willingness to pay. There are many reasons why people can believe that costs in general do not translate to costs to them in particular

There is no one to one correspondence between government expenditures and taxes. There is such a thing as a deficit. However, those expenditures have to be paid for somehow even in the case of a deficit. A deficit does not even delay in a real sense the costs of government expenditures. It is current resources that are used up in response to current government expenditures. The tax payment is delayed, but the real payment is not. Evidently, many are unaware or choose to ignore this obvious fact. There has been some attempt to correct for this problem. In 1999 every state besides Vermont had a balanced budget requirement (National Council of State Legislatures, 1999), though many had devised ways to circumvent the requirement. But if there were no tendency to ignore the cost associated with state expenditures, there would be no need for such a requirement.

Of course, U.S. government expenditures are not constrained by a balanced budget requirement. The attempts to impose a balanced budget amendment to the U. S. Constitution have come for the most part from advocates of reduced government spending. In 2011 the House voted on a balance budget amendment. It failed 261-165. (A two thirds vote was required.) 236 Republicans and 25 Democrats voted for the amendment, while 4 Republicans and 161 Democrats voted against it (Kasperowitz and Berman, 2001). The most obvious explanation for these results is that increased spending is more politically acceptable when it is financed by a deficit rather than by taxes. This implies that voters take costs of spending less into account when they are not associated with an increase in taxes. Since there is no reason to believe that voters overstate costs of spending when that spending is associated with increases in taxes, voters must be underestimating the costs of spending financed by a deficit.

Furthermore, many, if not most, environmental expenditures are not directly financed by government. Instead, they are foisted upon business by regulation. The resulting higher prices are not obvious to many, even though those are higher prices that they pay. Even in the case of taxes, there is the hope that somebody else, in particular the rich, will do most of the paying.

Finally, when it comes to government policy, most people have a one-track mind. They focus on one issue at a time. "If a good environment is a "goodie" let's have more of the stuff". Economists are among the few who sometimes insist on talking about trade-offs.

These problems of the first poll do not exist for the second poll which focuses on personal costs. People are forced to respond in terms of trade-offs. That is what household budgets are all about. There are obviously some irresponsible adults who ignore personal budget constraints, but they are far fewer than those who ignore government budget constraints, if those constraints exist. This is all part of the general rule that there is a serious cost to individuals if they make silly choices in their personal lives, while it is virtually cost free to the individual to make bad political choices.

Obviously, Sunstein does not agree with my interpretation of the two polls' results. Sunstein believes the pro-Kyoto poll reflects the true views of the poll's respondents, even though the "regardless of cost" clause makes no sense in a world of trade-offs. He believes that the second poll shows only that the respondents are not being adults about the issue of climate change. This interpretation does not make much sense to me. It just reflects Sunstein's own belief in the importance of climate change and that anybody who would agree with him is the adult in the room, though I doubt that he would accept the "regardless of cost" clause in that poll.

Sunstein could argue that respondents to the first poll were being altruistic, while respondents to the second poll were just being self-interested. However, respondents to each poll were drawn from the same population, so should have the same mix of altruists and the self-interested. Of course, the phrasing of polls can bring out different respondent characteristics. Sunstein's preference for the first poll's results is, in this interpretation, a preference for altruistic opinion compared to self-interested views. In our chapter on policy we question that preference when dealing with aggregate self-interest, as we are doing in this case.

Sunstein notes that the difference in poll results that we have been discussing in terms of environmental policy is not confined to polling results about that policy alone. In general, people are less willing to approve of government interferences with the market when they are confronted with the personal costs of so doing.

My interpretation of these results are also consistent with many of the findings of public finance. There is less opposition to indirect taxes than direct taxes because in the former case people are less aware that they are paying the tax, that is, they are less informed about the cost of government to them. Even when the taxes are direct, they are often assessed in a way that is less obvious to the tax payer. The tax payments are withheld by the employer, so the employee never sees the money that he is paying to the government.

It is interesting to note that Sunstein himself ignores these indirect taxes. In discussing the cost of climate change remediation he asserts that much of the financing can occur through a gasoline tax and so can be ignored. Whether an increase in the gasoline tax is a desirable means of financing government or not, spending the resulting receipts involves real costs because that expenditure uses up resources.

The Minimum Wage and Rent Control

There is additional evidence of the neglect of unintended consequences among people who should know better. Frey et al.,

1984, found that a majority of French and Austrian economists rejected both the proposition that the minimum wage generates unemployment among the less skilled and the proposition that rent control reduces the quantity and quality of housing. Economists from other countries accepted these propositions.

Frey et al. explained the French and Austrian economists' behavior in terms of values. They came from countries less sympathetic to markets. This is an explanation I accept. But both of these propositions about the labor and housing markets are valid or invalid independently of one's values. But the confirmation bias allows values to overwhelm the evidence even within a profession supposedly dedicated to truth.

In the other countries that Frey et al. examined a majority of economists found that the minimum wage reduced employment and that rent controls reduced the quality and quantity of housing. All these other countries were not as antithetical to markets as France and Austria. The Frey et al. explanation of this conflict among economists is that economists faced social environments which varied by country. Economists are susceptible to the political position of those around them –the old imitation game-- so one would expect the confirmation bias to produce more anti-market views among French and Austrian economists.

The most obvious alternative explanation does not hold water—that the effects of rent control and the minimum wage would be different in the French and Austrian economies. As far as these two propositions are concerned, the French and Austrian economies are substantially market economies. Even in those economies there are lots of firms in local markets hiring workers and lots of landlords renting housing so that differences in monopsonistic or monopolistic behavior cannot explain differences by countries in economists' answers.

Minimum wage laws are largely invariant country to country except for their amount relative to competitive wages for unskilled labor. In contrast, rent control laws can vary significantly in their details. One would not expect minimum wages to be less generous in France and Austria and, hence having less employment consequences. After all, France and Austria are significantly more effected by liberal ideology than the other countries. For the same reason one would not expect less restrictive rent controls in those two countries as well, though New York City is well known as possessing one of the most rigid rent control laws of all. That could explain the greater American economists' objections to rent control, but not the more favorable French and Austrian attitude.

A majority of French and Austrian economists did not believe that the minimum wage has negative effects on employment, while a majority of economists in the U.S., Germany and Switzerland had the opposite view. Combine this result with the fact that a majority of economists in all of these countries were in favor of the minimum wage. The inference was that political preferences were influencing the choices of the French and Austrian economists more than it influenced the others. Bear in mind that these French and Austrian economists were economists, the group most likely to know of the employment effect if they wanted to know. I know of no study of the views of other academics on these questions, but it would be surprising that they would be more aware of the unintended effects of either the minimum wage or rent control than economists, even French and Austrian economists.

Since the Frey et al. study there have been a large number of studies on the employment effect of the minimum wage. Some of these studies have shown no effect, but the Neumark and Washer (2008) survey of the literature concludes that the bulk of these studies show the expected negative effect. They argue that many of the "no effect" work suffers from not using a long enough time period for those effects to become manifest. A later work, (Mulligan, 2013), estimates that the employment loss generated by the minimum wage law changes from August 2009 to December 2010 was 829,000 workers.

Merline (2014) found that respondents' preference for the minimum wage changed from 87% to 77% when they were told that 500,000 jobs would be lost from an increase in the minimum wage. This number was the Congressional Budget Office estimate, a compromise between economists that believed in a big effect and those who believed in a negligible effect. This change in views of respondents suggests that many respondents were unaware of an employment effect before they were informed and that being thus informed will have an impact.

It should be noted that a majority of respondents did not change their preference for the minimum wage when informed of its employment effects. Since their friends were not informed, those friends were probably still in favor of the minimum wage. It would be costly to many respondents in terms of friendships lost to oppose the minimum wage.

This friendship effect makes the response to information always greater in the long-run than in the short-run. The reduced respondents' support for the minimum wage with increased information means that their friends are less likely to support the minimum wage even if they were not informed of the employment effect. The friendship effect produces a multiplier effect in the long-run. The survey procedure measures the effect of only one person knowing the unemployment effect of the minimum wage, since he does not know the other respondents or their reaction to the survey.

But there is another interpretation of the continued support of the minimum wage by some respondents. That the unintended results of the minimum wage are unfavorable does not imply that the total effect, including the intended effects, is unfavorable to some previously naïve voters. However, knowledge of the unanticipated effects causes some to change their minds. Later, we see how that weaker effect of unanticipated consequences has important policy implications.

Blinder and Krueger (2004) provide supportive evidence for the impact of knowledge about the employment effect to affect preferences for the minimum wage. In their 2003 United States survey they found that one of the most important variables determining opposition to a higher minimum wage was respondent's estimates of the impact of an increased minimum wage on the employment of those directly affected. Controlling for a host of relevant variables such as ideology and income, the higher that estimated effect the greater the opposition to higher minimum wages. They also found that a majority of respondents (57%) believed that there would be no effect, a position contrary to the bulk of evidence. That number probably understates the proportion of respondents that did not considered the employment effect of the minimum wage in determining their position on the minimum wage issue. The employment question is itself a prompt to their possibly being an employment effect, which many had probably not considered in approving the minimum wage.

It should be noted that this prompting effect could possibly explain the impact of knowledge about the employment effect of the minimum wage noted by Merline. Questioning about a possible impact tells respondents that there is such a possible impact. The different views of economists and other social scientists on the minimum wage's employment effect are probably less susceptible to this prompting effect. At the same time differences in the friendship pattern of the two groups would tend to capture the multiplicative effects of individual knowledge when shared by friendship groups.

Hoferkemp et al. (2009) provide additional evidence of knowledge about the employment effects of the minimum wage. They find that 74% of low education German voters, 77% of high education German voters, and 81% of German non-university social science teachers were in favor of the minimum wage, while only 15% of German economists approved. Even more interesting, 57% of both low and high education voters thought that the minimum wage reduced unemployment, while only 6% of economists thought so. To my knowledge, no serious study of the minimum wage has ever claimed that it reduced unemployment, though some studies have shown no effect I believe that respondents claiming a positive effect have no idea about the unemployment effect. Since they are in favor of the minimum wage, they attributed to it nothing but good qualities. They similarly claim that the minimum wage increases economic growth. (The Hoferkemp study does show an extremely low support by economists for the minimum wage compared to other surveys, but the differences between economists and others is so great that the possible sampling problem is not enough to explain that difference.)

Lack of information about the employment effects of the minimum wage is not the only relevant knowledge absence of minimum wage supporters. As in many other cases, they do not realize that costs imposed in business are dominantly paid for by consumers in the form of higher prices. This is a particular problem of the minimum wage, since the poor's consumption is more than averagely concentrated in products produced by minimum wage workers. Nor do minimum wage advocates consider the fact that a substantial portion of minimum wage beneficiaries come from higher income families. When MaCurdy (2015) looks at both, he finds that the minimum wage is a very ineffective way of redistributing income to the poor, far worse than the standard sales tax.

The price effect crucial to the MaCurdy analysis is ignored by naïve altruists in other situations. Many of my liberal friends refuse to shop at Walmart because it pays lower wages than many retail establishments. But they ignore the fact that the lower prices Walmart charges tend to benefit lower income shoppers in particular. This case is even a more dramatic example of the information deficiency of naïve altruists than the minimum wage case. The hiring policies of Walmart are also favorable to the poor. There is no balancing act required. Walmart pays less to its employees than some other retail establishments because it hires lower quality workers. Many retailers provide services to their customers that require better workers. Those workers provide information about product characteristics to customers, which requires them to have that knowledge to convey. Increasing the market for lower quality workers tends to reduce poverty. At least in terms of helping the poor, naïve altruists' boycott of Walmart is counterproductive. Their response to the lower wages of Walmart shows a total lack of information about how labor markets work. They start with the simple desire: "Wouldn't it be nice if wages were higher, especially the wages of lower income workers?" without considering the effects of putting that policy into action.

The Hoferkemp study shows a similar failure of respondents to consider unintended consequences in evaluating other interferences with the labor market. 75% of low education Germans, 58% of high education Germans, and 54% of social science teachers were in favor of limiting the salaries of high waged workers, while only 6% of German economists supported this proposal. The former threesome also thought that this proposal had the virtue of reducing unemployment, increasing growth and reducing the deficit.

Similar results were obtained about support for two other interferences with labor markets: retaining the current protections in Germany against dismissals and preventing profitable companies from dismissing workers, except that there was not quite a majority of social science teachers in favor of the latter. These results support our thesis about ignorance of unintended consequences. There is one more interesting result. Among all four of the groups of respondents the support for retaining the current protections in Germany against dismissal was much higher than the support for preventing profitable firms from dismissing workers. One possible explanation for this result is the status quo effect, that there is more support for an existing rule than for a new one.

The evidence detailed above is relevant to two propositions: one, that many people do not know about the unintended consequences of economic policy; two, that knowing those unintended consequences will reduce support for those policies. Other evidence provides additional support for the latter proposition. Page and Shapiro (1992) were able to explain all the substantial changes in aggregate preferences for economic policies by changes in the information that respondents received. Gerber and Karlin (2009) randomly gave some people the Washington Post, and randomly gave others the Washington Examiner. They found that the resulting changes in political preferences between the two groups of recipients was in the predicted direction.

A number of political scientists have examined the problem of political ignorance in a democracy, for example Kuklinsky et al. (2000). They conclude that political ignorance is a serious problem because most voters are woefully ignorant about most political facts. But they also frequently demonstrate that supplying some information such as the percent of the budget spent on a specific welfare program does not affect respondents' political choices.

There is an obvious interpretation of this latter result. The information being supplied is evidently not relevant to voter choices. But that does not imply that no information is relevant to those choices. Much political behavior involved in either providing information favorable to one's side or hiding unfavorable information makes no sense if it were not relevant to voter decisions. Often, the relevant information is about the unintended consequences of policies. Those politicians favoring greater spending try to hide the costs of that spending. Those opposed to greater environmental expenditures emphasize the costs of those expenditures. Campaign advertising would not be employed if propaganda or information were not effective.

CHAPTER 5

EVIDENCE OF THE GREAT DIVIDE

W e have argued that the divide between naïve altruists and the preferences of others is crucial to an understanding of political choices. One way of supporting that proposition is to show that some well-known relationships that are somewhat puzzling can be best explained by that divide.

The Role of Narrow Self-Interest

The public choice literature concentrates on the role of self-interest in determining political positions and there are features of political positions that do depend critically on narrow self-interest. The most obvious are the relationships between political party preferences and the following: income, union membership and membership in certain occupations such as business managers (Nelson and Greene, 2003). The Democratic Party has been the party advocating more income redistribution, more pro-union policies, and more anti-business policies. What the literature has not done is look at the role of self-interest in the context of the role of imitation, tradition, and altruism. In those terms increasing the role of self-interest among all interest groups should on the whole make a person more conservative if one holds tradition constant. Naïve altruism operates in the opposite direction, so an increase in self-interest would imply a reduced role for naïve altruism. Obviously, there are interest groups such as the poor that might very well become more liberal with an increased role of self-interest. But lumping all interest groups together that should not be the case. In the tests that follow we do not vary individuals by interest group, so for those implications the relevant self-interest is some aggregation of the self-interest of everybody.

In terms of the implications we examine, the biggest source of variation in the role of self-interest is between market behavior and political behavior. As discussed previously, people are less interested in their selves in their political choices because their individual political choices have virtually no impact on the policies that are actually adopted – the free-rider problem. But the test for that difference has to somehow control for another huge difference between market and political behavior – the role of externalities. People can have a self-interested reason for voting for costly reductions in external costs that they would not reduce through their market behavior. That proposition flows from the definition of external costs: costs that are not born by participants in a given market transaction, so people as voters might have a self-interest in reducing external costs that they do not have as market participants. The ideals of altruists that generate the big difference between political and market behavior are also based on externalities in one way or another. Environmentalism is the most obvious case. So controlling for externalities is no easy task. Fortunately, there are ways to distinguish between self-interest voting for externalities and altruistic voting for externalities. We will examine several of them.

Goodness at a Distance

If an individual has no narrow self-interested concerns with a decision, his own self-interest will be irrelevant to his decisions. Furthermore, to the extent that that individual associates only with other people that also have no self-interest concerns with that decision, even aggregate self-interest will be largely irrelevant. What else is left? Traditionalism and naïve altruism.

Focus for the moment on naïve altruism and the imitation of other naïve altruists. They will have more influence in any governmental decision where self-interest has less impact. Naïve altruists advocate greater environmental expenditures and regulation. On that account we would predict that non-local decisions would involve greater concern with the environment than local decisions.

But there are also traditional voters. Since environmentally oriented decisions have been growing in the United States and elsewhere, we would expect this group of voters to be more opposed to those decisions than the totality of others. We would also expect this group of voters to have less influence in local decisions because of the greater influence of self-interest in those decisions. I am unable to predict a priori how changes in the relative proportion of self-interested voters and traditionalists will affect the amount of environmental expenditures and regulation. However, we can predict that for exclusively locally impacted decisions, an increase in the importance of self-interest should have the same effect on environmental regulation however that effect manifests itself.

In confirmation of that prediction, Nelson and Greene (2003) have shown that in case after case national standards for environmental quality are stricter than local requirements when both the benefits and costs of environmental regulation are confined almost exclusively to localities. Obviously, those outside the locality will have a greater say in influencing national standards than they do in directly determining local standards, and they have less self-interest concerns with the local consequences of this class of regulation. Naïve altruism also explains why there are national standards at all for localized externalities. Oates and Schwab (1988) demonstrated that local governments will generate efficient environmental standards for these kinds of externalities. In contrast, national standards produce inefficient, one-size-fits-all regulation. But the national standards occur anyhow because they allow otherwise unconcerned citizens to feel good about doing their bit for a better environment.

More systematic tests involve comparing the political positions of the representatives of those localities directly affected by such regulation to the representatives of the localities not directly affected. ((Nelson and Greene, 2003) and Laband and Hussain (2005)). For each regulation, for example, the control of strip mining, desert protection and off-shore drilling, it is possible to test this proposition because of the large number of communities in each category. The test results are as predicted. In most of these cases the minor non-local costs of the regulation are greater than the minor non-local benefits, so something besides self-interest must explain this voting behavior. For example, the costs of restricting oil drilling in the National Wildlife Refuge (ANWAR) to non-Alaskans –higher gas prices and some reduction in Federal revenue—are greater than any benefits in better vistas of ANWAR, vistas that non-locals are unlikely to see in any case. But the opposition to oil drilling in ANWAR is dominantly non-Alaskan, as verified by the voting patterns of Congressmen and Senators on ANWAR.

Contrary to some of these tests, larger units are not always more liberal than their component units. The self-interest of the larger unit can be sufficiently harmed by more liberal behavior of its components. For example, the European Union has tried to place budgetary restrictions on its members in order to defend the general interests of the EU.

That does not imply that the EU is in general more conservative than its member states. Its Charter of Fundamental Freedom guarantees collective bargaining, no gender discrimination, and prohibits the death penalty (Bercusson, 2003). While these are the positions of all of the individual countries that make up the EU, these countries have not given these provisions the force of unchanging law in the same way as did the Charter.

Non-Use Value

The opposition to drilling in ANWAR is usually rationalized by positing a non-use or existence value to the amenities of ANWAR. Nonusers are supposedly altruistic toward users. Such an explanation has been used to rationalize a wide assortment of environmental policies. In surveys and in their political decisions people often choose environmental amenities for which they themselves have no use. Such a rationale seems particularly peculiar in the case of ANWAR when the users of the amenity – Alaskans – are in favor of oil drilling because they get benefits that more than compensate for the reduction in their amenities.

The altruistic explanation implies that people use the same utility calculation in determining non-use value that they use in other decisions. The calculations differ only because non-use value focuses on the utility of others. Diamond and Hausman (1993) have provided multiple tests showing that the way people calculate non-use value is inconsistent with utility maximization. They find, for example, that people are willing to pay approximately the same amount to save three specified wilderness areas as they are willing to pay to save any one of them. They are willing to pay approximately the same amount to save 200,000 birds as to save 2,000 of them. Furthermore, the amount they are willing to pay is affected by the order in which the amenity is listed.

These results are predictable from our model. Naïve altruism is displayed by how much one is willing to pay, not by what is accomplished. In terms of ideals, the more one is willing to pay for environmental amenities the better person one is considered to be. That explanation clearly works for the bird question. With respect to the order question, people are interested in demonstrating to the surveyor that they are good. If they demonstrate that goodness by a willingness to pay for one amenity, they can get away with paying less for other amenities.

There is another feature of non-use value. Willingness to pay (WTP) for a new amenity is consistently smaller than how much one would have to be recompensed if the same amenity, now an old amenity, were eliminated (WTA). This is predictable from our model. Tradionalism makes WTP higher than WTA.

The important messages of this section is that (1) ideals are based on something besides narrow self-interest even when that term is broadly enough defined to include altruism or animal love and (2) these ideals affect at least people's verbal behavior.

Age and Naïve Altruism vs. the Status Quo

That adults become more conservative as they age is well-known, and is documented in Inglehart et. al, 1998 and Nelson and Greene(2003) for example. But that relationship has usually been accepted without explanation. But there is a simple explanation expanding on the ideas we have previously developed.

Naïve altruism is seemingly an innate human preference. In addition, educators push the pro naive altruism agenda. As one ages in adulthood one has a longer time to be influenced by non-educators. Those influences can be of a mixed nature depending upon the social groups to which one belongs. On the average, however, that mixture must be more conservative than the education experience. We know that educators are more liberal than others, and that is particularly true of educators that discuss public policy. So the people a person deals with on the average are more conservative than their educators. In consequence, there should be positive relationship between age and conservatism.

In addition, as one ages there is the opportunity to find out through experience and contact with others the unintended consequences of naïve altruism. If a person takes advantage of those opportunities, he becomes more conservative. Highton (2009) finds that political knowledge increases with age when that political knowledge is measured by political facts not related to the consequences of policy alternatives. However, his results do show some indirect light on the aging effect on knowledge about the consequences of policy.

We make a less obvious prediction about the effects of aging. The effect of age on the college educated should be particularly strong. They are more strongly influenced by the most pronounced idealists, college teachers, when they are young. Even though they will tend to associate with fellow college graduates, they will also associate with higher income people. Though their associates are probably more liberal than others, they started from an even more liberal position. In consequence, they have more room to become more conservative as they age. As a result, the cross product of years of college and age has a significantly positive effect on conservative political positions even when both years of college and age are considered as other variables (Nelson and Greene (2003)).

Both observations -- the increased conservatism with age and the enhancement of that relationship by college education -- could be attributed in part to the cohort effect. In our case a cohort effect is produced because a person's political position is in part a function of his past associations. With the growth in government expenditures on liberal causes, a greater proportion of an older person's life has been spent in a smaller government era. That could explain at least part of the observed relationship between age and political positions. This cohort effect could also work for the particular age effect among the college educated because colleges have grown more liberal over time relative to the general population.

It should be noted that the cohort effect itself is predictable from our model. As we have seen, one of the determinants of voter positions is the pasts they have experienced. But since the pasts that they have experienced vary with age, political positions will vary by age – the cohort effect. Since there has been an increase over time in the amount of government activity, the past of older people makes them more conservative.

There is an alternative explanation for an age-conservative relationship. Sapolsky (2014) maintains that the pre-frontal cortex is not fully formed in young adults. Among other results, this tends to make them more empathetic than older adults. Furthermore, the less developed pre-frontal cortex produces less intellectual control over emotions, a phenomenon that would help insure that the resulting greater altruism of young adults would be of the naïve kind.

Since the age-conservative relationship is so strong both our and Sapolsky's processes could operate at the same time. Furthermore, there are ways of distinguishing between Sapolsky's explanation and ours. His does not predict a cohort effect and ours does

We would also predict that people should become less liberal with age throughout their lifetime. They are continuously being affected by their group to overcome their initial naïve liberalism. Sapolsky's age-conservative relationship depends upon a single lifetime event—the development of the frontal cortex. That event is over by the age of thirty or earlier. Any additional movement toward conservatism cannot be so explained.

There is a problem with testing this proposition. It is in the self-interest of older voters to support the maintenance of Social Security and the Democratic party is closely identified with that cause. For the 2008 and 2012 elections the Social Security issue was relatively less important than in other elections. For those two elections Republican support increased with age well beyond 30 years of age (Gallup,2013). For earlier elections that did not seem to be the case. In Sapolsky's defense the big drop off by age in the change in Democratic support in the 2008 and 2012 elections was right after the age of thirty.

If we focus on particular issues other than Social Security rather than party support, the case for the continual growth in conservative support with age is increased. Nelson and Greene

(2003) regressed support for many issues such as welfare, education and the environment with a quadratic age function. The results did not show that the age effect was greater at younger ages. The test for that proposition was simply looking at the slope of the age squared term. The Sapolsky proposition predicts a slope of that term in the liberal direction. For eight issues excluding social security that prediction held, but for eight other issues it did not. Even for the issues that conform to the Sapolosky prediction, the age at which the regression produces an overall liberal effect is on the whole far greater than the lifespan of most of the respondents, somewhat greater than 30 years of age.

Religion

Professors are not the only preachers of social ideals. Preachers engage in that activity as well. Some of the two groups' preaching is about the same set of ideals – aid to the poor, the sick, education, and the environment. After all, many church charities are focused on those activities, and "social justice" is the theme of much church sermonizing. However, professors are not known for preaching morality nearly to the extent that religions do. That activity was pre-empted by religion and professors are notably non-religious (Gross and Simmons (2007)). So the church is a source of social ideals, but a broader set of ideals than those emanating from colleges. For the ideals that they have in common – social justice and the environment – church sermons would tend to make their audiences more liberal.

But churches provide more than a venue for sermons. They are also a source of socializing. Church going and related activities are one of the principal forms of community involvement for many Americans. Churches both create a lot of associations and attract people who want a lot of associations. Depending on their character, associations can make one either more liberal or conservative. But, as we have seen in the section on age, on average they tend to make one more conservative. They provide a counterweight to the liberalism generated by innate altruism and education. In consequence, the socializing associated with churches should generate more conservatism. This process is amplified by many liberals disdain for churchgoing.

The evidence shows that this community involvement effect is far stronger than the opposite effect of church sermonizing for economic issues. It is well known that those who attend church more frequently are more likely to vote for Republicans. However, that association is usually attributable to the abortion issue. But, as shown by Nelson and Greene (2003), church attendance increases conservatism with respect to most of the items on the liberal agenda, not just abortion. Church attendance is significantly associated with greater conservatism on welfare, health, education, environment, social security, parks, defense expenditures, and conservatism, Republicanism, voting for President, and abortion. The first seven of these categories are unrelated to abortion preferences. Church attendance is significantly positively related to one item on the liberal agenda, expenditures to aid Blacks. That might be attributable to the sermonizing effect. The probability of seven out of eight results in the same direction due to chance is less than .05. Furthermore, for all of the issues unrelated to abortion, there are no significant differences in the effect of attendance by major religions. Sermons do not seem to count for much outside of abortion.

There is another explanation for the association of church attendance with political conservatism. Religious people are more conservative. One of the most important reasons for church attendance is that was what one's parents did. There is the obvious close relationship between people's faith and the faith of their fathers and mothers. Church attenders are traditionalists. As discussed earlier, this traditionalism in personal behavior is associated with traditionalism in political behavior.

The conservative role of religion in the United States might be one of the explanations for the greater conservatism of the United States compared to Western Europe. Church attendance is so much higher in the United States. The resulting greater community involvement should make the United States more conservative than Europe.

City Size

It is well known that liberalism increases with increases in city size. I believe the process that produces this result is a variant of the ancient economic principle: "Specialization is limited by the size of the market." The larger the city size the more one can specialize in one's friends. One chooses friends in part either because they have similar political views or because they have characteristics similar to one's own that are highly correlated with political views. In either case their political views will have less impact on one's own views in large cities because one does not have to adjust one's views very much to conform. Look at the special case of associates with exactly the same political views as oneself before any conforming adjustment. There will be no conforming adjustments to that set of friends because none is required. But if the person and his friends have already had their views influenced by conformity, that past conformity will still operate. However, we have seen that the influence of conformity cumulates over one's life. So sufficiently specialized friendship groups formed at an earlier age will be less impacted on the average by later conformity than others. Furthermore, as we have seen, the character of early conformity can be quite different than later conformity because younger people and their associates are more liberal. Think, for example, of college graduates imbued by their professors with ideals. In large cities they can stick together. There is, then, less social pressure to revise those ideals.

We saw in the section on "Age" that the conformity effect was on the whole toward conservatism to counter the liberalizing effect of innate altruism and education. The reduction in this effect with increases in population density implies that there will be more naïve altruistic voters than other voters in larger cities compared to smaller cities.

There is an alternative hypothesis that could explain part of the city size effect. Holsey and Borcherding (1996) maintain that in larger cities a person has less of a social network to fall back upon in case of some disaster because a larger proportion of them are migrants and family size is smaller. In consequence, they are more in favor of insurance by way of the government. Out of five city size categories, with rural as the dummy variable, all five significantly advocate greater welfare expenditures, one significantly favors more health expenditures, and one advocates more expenditures on social security (Nelson and Greene (2003)). Also, there are other issues where self-interest is closely associated with city size. Four significantly want greater aid to large cities than rural areas wish, five significantly want more mass transit, two significantly want greater expenditures to fight crime, and one significantly wants more parks.

However, residents of larger cities are in favor of other parts of the liberal agenda that are neither related to social insurance nor the other issues of direct self-interest to cities. Four city size categories significantly favor abortions relative to rural area; four significantly want greater expenditures on the environment, three significantly want greater educational expenditures, two are significantly against more defense expenditures, and two significantly want greater aid to Blacks among white respondents. Furthermore, the larger the city the greater are these effects. Obviously these results cannot be explained in terms of a social insurance hypothesis.

Furthermore, the impact on liberalism of city size when one was sixteen is as great as current city size. Past city size does not affect current self-interested preferences for social insurance, but it does affect the socializing process.

This impact of city size is another reason the United States is more conservative than Western Europe. A smaller proportion of the population of the United States is concentrated in big cities with their smaller community involvement effects.

Putnam (2000) found that the overall community involvement effect is greater in the United States than Europe. He used as his measure the standard measures of social capital – trust and organizational membership.

Internationalism

One of the important differences between ideals and the advocacy of the status quo is in the medium of their transmission. The media play a central role in the transmission of ideals. Word of mouth is more important relatively in the advocacy of the status quo. The media communicate at greater distances than word of mouth. There is, indeed, an international market for ideals. We would, therefore, expect that liberal altruistic voters will have more of an international perspective than others.

For evidence, Inglehart et. al, 1998 examined answers to the question, "Which of these geographic groups would you say you belong to first of all?" Respondents are given three options: (1) "The world as a whole or the continent/subcontinent", (2) "The country as a whole", (3) "The locality or town in which one lives." They find that the younger, the more educated, and leftists each had a significantly higher proportion of cosmopolites compared to their opposite counterparts. Those results are consistent with our prediction. But in the only city size comparison in Inglehart , Russians had a significantly greater proportion of cosmopolites than Moscovites, a result inconsistent with our prediction. When a similar question is asked, "How proud are you to be a citizen of your country?" Russians are significantly prouder than Moscovites, and all the other comparisons hold.

Further evidence consistent with the theory is provided by a comparison between professorial behavior as provided by Gross and Simmons (2007) and the Inglehart data. Thirty eight percent of professors in the United States regarded themselves primarily as citizens of the world (as opposed to citizens of towns, states and regions, and nations) while 19% of all United States respondents had the same international perspective (Inglehart et. al, 1998), a significant difference. This 38% for professors is far higher than any of the percentages associated with any of the categories in the Inglehart study, a clear indication of how big a relative role ideals play in determining professors' political positions.

Variation in the Status Quo

Tradition does not necessarily operate in support of free markets. Rather it increases the role of the status quo. If in the past the economy were more socialist and egalitarian, those in favor of the past would be more opposed to free markets. Then, in the former Soviet Union and prior to the rule of Putin, the greater community involvement, the greater the support for income equality as opposed to incentives for individual effort. Inglehart et. al, 1998 et. al, 1998 provides support for that prediction. Moscow was significantly more in favor of incentives for individual effort than Russia. (78 vs.63 percent), while in the United States large cities are more liberal than any other city size category. Similarly, in countries that had recently experienced Communism, younger people were significantly more in favor of greater incentives for individual effort than older people relative to countries that had not. In Russia, for example, the percentages were 64 and 52 respectively. In the United States the differences were significantly in the other direction. (57 and 63 percent). Similar results occur when the question is whether there should be more or less state ownership. Of course, these age results can also be explained by the cohort effect, but, as discussed earlier, the simplest explanation for that cohort effect is also the status quo effect.

The status quo effect can be examined explicitly. Inglehart et. al, 1998 et al. asks their respondents to choose between radical social reform, moderate reform, or keeping things the way they are. 34% of Russians chose the last option as opposed to 25% of Moscovites. In 34 countries older people were more in favor of that option than younger adults, while in 6 countries those results were reversed. In total 22% of older people chose the option while only 14% of younger adults did so. (All these results are statistically significant.) These results are independent of the nature of the economy of the countries involved. Both the city-size and the age results are predictable from the community involvement impact on traditionalism.

A Slippery Slope?

Naïve altruism and advocacy of the status quo have a common characteristic that can have a significant effect on the time path of policy. The behavior that they generate is a function of where policy is and has been in the past. That by definition is the case for status quo desires. But it is true for naive altruism as well. The standard way that people reveal that they have ideals is by advocating "more" – more environmental expenditures or a greater redistribution of income, say. That is the way survey questions are almost invariably phrased. There is a great advantage to this way of communicating ideals. One does not have to know the present degree of progressivity in taxes or how large environmental expenditures are or the desired amount of those expenditures. Just that if one answers, "more", one is on the side of the idealists. There is a substantial literature focused on how little voters know about these and similar facts, for example Kuklinski et al. (2000). But there is a reason for that political ignorance. Those are not the facts that voters would use even if they had them as evidenced by their not using such facts when given to them. We have already seen that voters use information when they deem it relevant.

Both ideals and traditionalism generate a lagged response to any increase in government expenditures. The initial increase in government expenditures increases the level of expenditures associated with more expenditures and it would lessen the traditionalist's resistance to that new level of expenditures because it would be closer to the current level.

Self-interest also produces some lagged response. Current interest groups have more impact on policy than potential interest groups. An increase in government expenditures creates more beneficiaries of government largesse, and some of those who have been harmed by that policy have been eliminated as current interest groups. In consequence, the self-interest resistance to any level of government expenditures is somewhat diminished by higher levels of past government expenditures.

However, one would not expect this process to go on indefinitely. Self-interest, is in part a function of the level of government expenditures. As those expenditures increase relative to those in the aggregate self-interest of voters, one would expect self-interested voters to increase their opposition to those expenditures. Clearly, that statement holds if self-interested voters determined their votes by the difference between the actual level of expenditures and their desired level. But one would also expect that statement to hold even if self-interested voters focused on the proposed change in government expenditures that was against their interest. We have previously introduced the concept of "deadweight loss", the amount of money people are willing to spend to get to an optimal level of expenditures. We can also talk about a change in deadweight loss in comparing two non-optimal states. Look at what happens for nearly all reasonable supply and demand curves. The further both are from an optimal state, the greater the change in deadweight loss for any given difference between the two. (See the Appendix.) So even if self-interested voters only responded to the change in the self-interested impact of any legislation, that opposition would increase the higher the level of government expenditures. Fully informed altruism would also cause voters to respond to the level of government expenditures, though we do not believe that that is currently a major source of voter preferences. So the level of government expenditures would count in determining votes. In other words, there should be an equilibrium level of government expenditures associated with given values of our underlying parameters.

But, of course, the values of those parameters can change systematically over time. Those parameter changes go a long way to explaining the increases in government expenditures over time. The increase in the college educated increases the role of naïve altruism. At the same time community involvement has declined. As noted by Putnam (2000), there has been a decline in the two most frequently used social capital variables, trust and organizational membership where that membership involves social contact. This decline in social capital can be attributed in part to a decline in church attendance, increases in city size, an increase in migration, and the advent of television.

Conclusion

This chapter has tried to show that the divide between naive altruistic voters and their foes explains a lot of the variation in voter preferences known as the conservative liberal divide. It provides some justification for focusing on that difference in discussing good economic policy.

CHAPTER 6

POLICY

Policy recommendations are normative statements. They require some idea about what constitutes good outcomes—value statements--as well as behavioral propositions about the consequences of various policies. Is there a way to determine whether a value statement is valid or invalid? The logical positivists such as Ayer (1936) say, "No". This is a rather uncomfortable conclusion. Of necessity society makes policy decisions all the time, and those policy decisions require values. If the values themselves are arbitrary, what is the point of any investigation of the consequences of policy in terms of those values?

This problem has generated two different responses from economists. One response is to accept the positivist's position. "We will just specialize in the knowledge game, and leave the values to others." The problem with that response is that many of the others have not done well in the value statement job. Policy recommendations are all askew as a result.

The other response is a non-response. "We will continue with the utilitarian values we used long before the positivist's questioning of value statements arose." In the ensuing pages I provide a defense to much of this approach, but even at best this approach is incomplete. Utilitarian policy statements require an aggregation of individual utilities and an appropriate aggregation requires its own defense.

Of course, the problem of appropriate values is not a problem confined to economists. Values are the meat and potatoes of philosophers. Many modern philosophers reject the positivists' position. Disparate philosophers such as Rawls (1990), Nozick (1974) and Walzer (1983) have adopted positions inconsistent with the views of the positivists. But how is it possible to get around the "arbitrary values" charge of the positivists? One way to do so is to assert "Appropriate values are the values that people want." Or one might say "Determine the values that people want when they are acting impartially." So some have tried just that by asking people their policy preferences usually on issues where the respondents have no self-interest (Konow, 2003). They usually feel that these actual preferences have some relationship to the values that people should have – moving from the positive to the normative. Other philosophers such as Rawls intuit what people would want if they were given more information about their wants. There is some basis for such intuitions. Philosophers do, indeed, have some idea about human preferences based on their own preferences and those of their associates. But do these preferences represent in some sense the preferences of humanity in general? The fact that philosophers start with such disparate value assumptions suggest that at least some of their intuitions are wrong.

A minority of philosophers adopt a different position. There is a basic human nature, and preferences can be judged by how well they satisfy that nature. Arnhart (1998) is the most explicit advocate of that position. It is still possible, however, to object on the positivist's grounds that one can still not move from is to ought.

I accept the Arnhart view, but provide a rationale that does not require any value assumption. People choose what they want compared to the alternatives available and given the information they possess. That holds for both personal choices and choices about appropriate social rules. If they had enough information, their choices would indicate what they really wanted. For the purpose of giving people what they wanted, "good" can be defined in a non-arbitrary way: what people wanted if they had enough information.

People often seek advice about their choices. The advice they want is how best to achieve what they want. That, for example, is how the patient-doctor relationship works. Its success depends upon a reasonable amount of agreement that people want health, a concept upon which there is also a reasonable amount of agreement. The agreement is not perfect – the sometimes conflict between quality of life and longevity, say. But it is close enough to make doctor's advice useful.

In this context "good" is defined as what people would want if they had enough information. One could also define "good" in an abbreviated way and get to the same definition. "Good" is simply that which people want. By their behavior people indicate their preference for decisions with better information. That preference, of course, does not imply an unlimited purchase of information, since information involves substantial acquisition and processing costs. But, holding costs constant, the more information the better. This definition of "good" boils down to a tautology. For the purpose of giving people what they want, "good" could be defined as that which people want. The tautological nature of this definition of "good" is important. As long as the purpose clause of this definition is either explicitly stated or implicit, no value assumptions are required in this definition of "good".

There are two important caveats. First, people are sometime resistant to new information if it requires them to abandon their most cherished views, the well-known confirmation bias. But that does not prevent them from accepting the general proposition – "the more information the better". The confirmation bias is deplored in general even by those who display it in a particular case. The pejorative status of the term "confirmation bias" is suggested by its name. Biases of whatever nature are considered "bad" because they get in the way of using information to its fullest.

The second caveat is that "more information" requires some elaboration. Information is multidimensional. Even a single policy choice involves a multitude of consequences. Increases in information in some dimensions can be associated with decreases in others. Furthermore, more information is better measured by how close it is to the information required to make informed decisions than by the more obvious measure – the amount of information relative to no information.

It is this second consideration that makes altruism so problematic. The altruist probably knows less about unintended consequences than either traditionalists or the self-interested because of the confirmation bias that tends to make altruists naïve. But, even more importantly, altruists have to know more to make appropriate decisions. They have to know about the unintended consequences of policy that affect others because those consequences are relevant to their policy decisions and they are not relevant to either the traditionalists or the self-interested.

The college experience represents both those sources of problems with the standard knowledge measure. People learn a lot about, political choices in college, but at the same time they are more likely to become naïve altruists, a reduction in information relative to required information in another dimension. In consequence, one cannot say without further evidence whether going to college increases or decreases political information. If, however, we restrict ourselves to unambiguous cases of information increases, then it is likely that increases in information increase the likelihood that people make better choices.

Our definition of the "good" conflicts in part with the standard focus on impartial decisions. The decisions of which they and we are concerned are decisions about desirable social rules. Self-interest is a big component of those decisions. Instead of trying to eliminate that component from decisions, we recognize that such decisions require an appropriate aggregation of individual decisions.

Take, for example, the standard preference, "I want more for myself and my family." That is not an impartial preference, and in operation it can lead to others having less. But that need not be the case with an appropriate aggregation of preferences with others having a role in the distributive decision. To eliminate individual preference on the grounds that it is not impartial would be to eliminate an important human desire from determining appropriate social rules. Not all individual desires for more lead to a comparable reduction in the amount available to others. The economy is not simply a zero sum game.

Still, there are experiments focused on distributional issues and without aggregation. In those cases it makes sense to confine the experiments to impartial decisions. In doing so, however, one has to recognize that that is a rather narrow class of decisions. The quest for impartiality has in part been motivated by a desire to avoid problems associated with the aggregation of preferences. Some of the advocates of impartiality believe that with impartial judgments all might have the same preference so no aggregation is required. But our previous chapters suggest that people will still have different preferences, so aggregation is required in any case. We will examine issues raised by the aggregation of preferences in the next chapter.

Instead of the impartiality requirement, I define "good" as how the defining group would define it if it had enough information. Then, for purposes of giving the group what it wants with enough information, "good" is defined as that which would give the group what it wanted if the individuals within the group had enough information. The tautological nature of the definition of "good" remains.

What's the point of such a tautology? One can easily think of other ways to define "good". "Good is what God wants". "Good is the greatest number of species" etc. These other definitions either have insuperable problems of implementation or are arbitrary in the sense that most people would reject such definitions. But certainly the latter objection could not hold for our definition of the "good." People clearly want what they want.

Obviously a lot of problems exist. What does, "what a group wants" mean? What size group? Though individuals are the ultimate actors, groups of individuals do make decisions. That requires an aggregation of individual preferences in some way. Sometimes the group has some formal aggregation process in rules of governance. Sometimes the group arrives at some consensus in determining its mores. "What a group would want if it had enough information" is simply the laws and mores that the group decides with that amount of information. Information can affect both what individuals want and the way in which individuals decide on how their preferences should be aggregated.

The crucial difference between this approach and other social contract theories is the "with enough information" clause. It would be hard to argue with the appropriateness of that clause, since people by their behavior indicate that they believe decisions with more information are better than decisions with less information, though the improvement might not be worth the costs of greater information. And such a clause would tend to make our value statement more acceptable to non-social contract philosophers. Nearly all philosophers believe that their own approach to values would be accepted if people knew enough.

This likely consensus comes at a price. No preferred policy positions follow immediately from our value tautology. But preferred policy positions do follow from the tautology plus testable propositions about human preferences. Some positions follow rather easily from generally accepted propositions. Some require empirical propositions less widely accepted. The problem lies with the "with enough information" clause in our value tautology. The task of finding out what values people have at any given moment is relatively straightforward. Just ask them or devise circumstances in which these values are revealed. And that is what scholars have done. They realize that self-interest as well as values affects decisions. They try to control for self-interest by either looking at cases in which respondents have no self-interest (Konow, 2003) or by instructing respondents to ignore their self-interest (Rawls, 1990). They find three driving principles: need, efficiency, and equity (benefits should be related to inputs.). But (Miller, 1992) find that the weights given to these principles in determining decisions varies by societies. This latter result, well known before Miller, has led to the position of the social relativists (Walzer, 1983), that societies can only be judged by their own values.

But determining the values that people have at a moment does not determine what values they would have if they had enough information. That problem cannot be directly handled in this world of limited information. But none the less relevant evidence can be obtained. Vary the information and see how values change.

Conceivably, values are impervious to information, that people combine information about consequences with their own underlying values to determine their policy positions. However, Froehlich et al. (1987) show that people's values are, indeed, affected by at least one form of information, information about what others value. One suspects that other forms of information would also be relevant.

Cultural Relativism and Innate Preferences

Cultural relativism is built on a fundamental insight. People's values are determined in large part by the values of their culture. However, cultural relativism ignores another fact. Though culture affects wants, so does biology. There are such things as innate preferences, though they need not dominate in any culture at any given time. There is, for example, an innate preference for health, holding cost constant. Christian Scientists might disagree, so their preferences would not coincide with a full application of this innate preference criterion. As argued by scholars such as Pinker (2002), people, whether they are Trobriand or Manhattan Islanders, have their humanity in common, enough to generate some common innate preferences.

The big difference between innate preferences and culturally determined preferences is that the former is fixed in the absence of genetic engineering and the latter is variable at least in the long run. That something is fixed is essential in determining what people want. If, for example, people had no fixed preferences in the broadest sense, then there would be no way of determining whether one set of social rules was better than another. We know that cultures are variable because they vary. That opens the possibility that cultural rules can be improved by moving toward those that better serve innate preference. As Fukuyama (2011) points out, that is exactly the position of assorted political philosophers, Aristotle, Plato, Hobbes, Rousseau and Locke. They distinguish between nature and convention or law. A just city had to exist in conformity with man's permanent nature.

This is simply a problem in constrained maximization. The constraint is what is fixed –innate preferences. In the short run even social rules have a constraining, but not perfectly constraining, role. Even if a person knew that an extant rule was unsatisfactory by the innate preference criterion, he might very well be in favor of that rule because others were in favor. However, it is likely that information about the inferiority of a current cultural rule should reduce at least somewhat a person's enthusiasm for that rule. If enough members of a group acquire that information, that group's view could change to better serve innate preferences. Innate preferences can rule in the long run but would have a hard time doing so in the short run when competing with current social rules.

How does one determine whether a particular social rule is inferior to some other social rule? That question can only be answered by some knowledge about innate preferences. Maximizing in terms of innate preferences is not a return to a "state of nature." Contrary to Hobbes and Rousseau, man did not start out with innate preferences that were then changed by social rules. Man has always been imbedded in society. Indeed, one of man's innate preferences is the preference for social interaction. Still, the behavior of primitive man is important in determining innate preferences. What makes the preferences of primitive man of particular interest is that most of man's innate preferences were largely formed at those earlier times in response to survival pressures at those times.

Innate Preferences

One of the problems with dealing with innate preferences is specifying what those innate preferences are. As we have previously argued, there is evidence for innate preferences for self-interest, altruism, equity, and conformity. The latter has no effect by itself. Its impact is to make an individual's preferences dependent in part on the operation of the innate preferences of others. However, each of the other innate preferences can lead to policy preferences which are different from the preferences produced by the others. For example, equity would often lead to approving the market generated distribution of income while altruism pushes for a more equal distribution.

To complicate the problem even further, Haidt (2012) argues that people will differ innately in their mix of these innate preferences. Identical twins tend to have more similar political preferences than fraternal twins. Not all of that result is directly attributable to genetics because genetics also help determine the social groups one joins, which in turn helps determine ones politics.

However, we can still say what happens to political preferences as information increases. By definition, information should not change innate preferences. So holding the mix of innate preferences constant, we can determine what information does to the political preferences generated by each innate preference in turn.

We have already seen what happens to the liberal altruistic voter. For the most part he is naïve. He does not take into account the unintended consequences of his policy preferences and those unintended consequences tend to be unfavorable in terms of the self-interest of most people. An increase in information would have the liberal altruistic voter take those consequences into account. That need not change the minds of all liberal altruistic voters. There are still the direct consequences of the policies they favor because of those direct consequences. But marginal liberal altruistic voters are likely to change their views as a result of knowledge of the substantially unfavorable effects of these unintended consequences. We have seen this process work in the case of preferences for the minimum wage. Knowledge about the impact of the minimum wage on the unemployment of covered workers had a substantial negative effect on support for that proposed legislation.

Of course, before a naïve altruist takes unintended consequences into account, he has to accept the proposition that a policy should be judged by its consequences rather than the intentions of its advocates. As discussed in Chapter 2, the stated intentions of politicians are often used in determining votes. But we also argued there that these intentions were used as a predictor of the consequences of the candidate's actions if elected. When new knowledge of those consequences goes against the intention's prediction of those consequences, there will be a reduced preference for good intention candidates. In Chapter 2 we found evidence that new information about unintended consequences reduced support for naïve altruists' policies. That is also evidence that some "intention" voters change their preferences when confronted by this information. I know of no "good intention" candidate that ever admits that the consequences of his policies would have unfavorable total consequences as the electorate would so judge those consequences. As far as public policy is concerned, it is the consequences of those policies rather than the intentions of the policy makers that are relevant. Policy makers only affect the great majority of others through the consequences of their policies. With enough information the polity would recognize that fact and act accordingly. As previously indicated, many base their vote on how empathetic a candidate is rather than the consequences of his policy. That empathy comes largely from supporting the agenda of the naïve voter. Moving from focusing on empathy to focusing on consequences would tend to make a voter less naïve.

In contrast to naïve altruists, greater information need not change the votes of self-interested voters. They already were voting against the liberal altruistic policies. However, the vigor of their opposition to those policies might increase. But even in that case we would expect smaller effects from these voters than from liberal altruistic voters. They are more likely to already know of these unfavorable indirect consequences. The confirmation bias does not discourage them from such knowledge.

How about two of the major determinants of voting – imitation and traditionalism? To the extent that a voter is imitating the votes of others based on their self-interest, their vote will change in the same way self-interested voters change. To the extent that the voter is imitating previously naive altruistic voters he will vote less like those voters because some of those voters will be less naïve. To the extent that a voter is a traditionalist, his vote will change because the traditions have changed. Fewer liberal altruistic voters means that the status quo will be less favorable to liberal altruistic policies.

All of the processes we have examined point in a single direction. With enough information liberal altruism will have less effect on policy than it has currently. But there might be another issue. Will enough information change the mix of altruism, imitation, self-interest, and traditionalism in some systematic way? Each of these preferences are to some extent innate (Haidt,2012) but can be modified by culture. What kind of modifications would we expect through increases in knowledge?

However, voters have no particular incentive to acquire more political information than they already have. Voting is just an extension of conversations. On the information front we can hope that better information is used with purveyors of that information having the incentive to provide that better information if they have it. Under those conditions, there is no reason to expect the weights that people use between tradition, self-interest, and altruism to change. The big change will still be the changes to the character of altruism.

But altruists could prefer policies that would be determined by democratic decisions, but decisions where voters use the maximum amount of information rather than simply the amount they have an incentive to acquire. One could argue that traditionalism will be reduced by knowledge increases. A blind acceptance of traditions seems inconsistent with an inquiring mind. That is one of the reasons why universities are so liberal. A little reason might well reduce the role of traditionalism, but look at the way that reason is practiced.

Multiculturalism is one of the current fashions in universities. As practiced, it does not seem to be intellectually coherent, but has a coherent political message. For the most part multiculturalists are cultural relativists. Each culture must be judged in its own terms. At the same time, the multiculturalists condemn Western capitalism, which is not judging it in its own terms. The following argument gives some coherence to this seeming inconsistency. There are other traditions beside capitalism that have been used by various societies. So there is nothing sacrosanct about the tradition of capitalism. But, of course, capitalism is the dominant ,tradition in our country, and a cultural relativist would have to accept it as such. But most multiculturalists do not accept it, though they are willing to use the cultural relativist argument in defending non-capitalist societies. The multi-culturists provide no solid way to make cultural comparisons. At best they fall back on naïve altruism.

This substitution of naive altruism for traditionalism is based on the first responses of an inquiring mind, but this little knowledge might well be inconsistent with responses based on enough information. In substance Hayek (1988) makes that case, though in different terms. The traditions in the Western World have worked in terms of providing people a good life. But many people are unaware of the role of free-markets and the family in giving people what they want.

Neither the free-market nor the nuclear family came about by any reasoned process. Nobody voted to establish free-markets or the primacy of the family. These institutions worked in terms of group survival. Individuals have an incentive to trade. Societies that allowed them to do so prospered compared to societies that did not. This both encouraged the spread of free markets and made most individuals better off as a result. But the absence of popular support in generating free markets makes such institutions fragile. That free markets are based on greed condemn them in the eyes of many. It requires more than a modicum of information to understand the virtues of markets. Naïve altruists do not possess such information. The substitution of naive altruism for tradition in this context hardly produces the better results that would occur with enough information. This is the result of the multidimensional character of information and measuring information in terms of the required information to make appropriate choices. The greater information of the inquiring mind is associated with the lack of information about the unintended consequences of the naïve altruist, information that altruism requires. To that extent I agree with Hayek

But our analysis differs markedly from that of Hayek on other counts. He maintains that instincts have gotten in the way of the development of the tradition of free markets. In particular, the instinct of xenophobia has been an impediment, since intertribal trade was probably the first developed trade. But xenophobia is not the only innate preference. It is in terms of the other innate preferences that Hayek implicitly approves of free-markets. Innate preferences are often in conflict. In this case xenophobia conflicts with self-interest, another innate preference. I maintain that such conflicts can only be resolved by increases in information. In fact, more information has pushed more people to advocate free trade. The Law of Comparative Advantage did not come from tradition itself.

One of the problems with a reliance on tradition as an appropriate basis for policy is that the world changes over time. The traditions that produced social survival in one era might not generate that survival in another. One of the obvious changes over time has been the increase in population density. That increase tends to generate greater externalities. One's actions tend to have a greater effect on others the closer the physical contact. For example, potential pollution problems are greater now than they were at earlier times in man's history. However, it is conceivable that the political process is such that the response to these new problems produces worse results than no response at all. Given the current importance of naïve altruism, that is certainly a possibility. However, there is at least hope that that naivety can be reduced. Indeed, that is what Hayek is trying to do, though he does not say so. He maintains that tradition trumps reason, but he is using reason in that argument and hopes that readers will accept his reasons. He says that value statements cannot be validated. Yet he says that abandoning tradition produces famine and other disasters. Obviously, he believes that is unfortunate and expects his readers to share that assessment if they accept his analysis. In fact, he is using the same sort of values that I use at the same time that he argues against the validity of any values.

An increase in information is also likely to increase altruism relative to self-interest. The more information a person possesses, the more likely he will have information about the world in general compared to narrowly focused information about a person's specific situation. Local newspapers tend to have local news, but that news is about people in a broader set of circumstances than the specific circumstances of any one individual. National news on TV is news about an even wider set of people. This broader set of informational inputs as information increases will produce a broader set of outputs as far as conversation is concerned, and voting preferences are just an extension of conversational preferences.

However, just as in the traditions versus altruism case, the altruism that tends to replaces the self-interest is a flawed kind of altruism. In consequence, it is not clear that this improves political choices.

The conclusions of this analysis comes very close to that of Friedman in his famous Essays in Positive Economics (1953). The source of much disagreement about policy is lack of information. Naïve altruist will disagree less with others if they were to become less naïve –a function of information. However, that disagreement will not totally disappear because there remain differences in innate preferences and circumstances. We still have to deal with those differences.

There are, however, important differences between our analysis and that of Friedman. Friedman's assertions about the role of information to reduce policy disagreements is a positive proposition rather than a normative one. Our view about the role of information flows from our basic normative tautology. In order to give people what they want, decisions with more information are likely to be better decisions than those with less information. Not only should there be more consensus with more information, but that consensus decision is likely to be better in a normative sense.

That that is not implied by Friedman becomes clear when one realizes that he is using a different value assumption – "Maximize liberty". The Friedmans quote with approval John Stuart Mill (Friedman and Friedman, 1990).

"The sole end for which mankind, individually or collectively, in interfering with the liberty of action of any of their number, is self-protection. The only purpose for which power can be rightfully exercised over any member of a civilized community, against his will, is to prevent harm to others. His own good, either physical or moral, is not enough warrant....The only part of the conduct of any one, for which he is amenable to society, is that which concerns others. In the part which merely concerns himself, his independence is, of right, absolute. Over himself, over his own body and mind, the individual is sovereign."

This statement of Mill and the Friedmans is a far stronger statement than our value tautology. People who agree with giving people what they want with enough information might very well disagree with the Friedman position. Some people are in favor of banning cigarettes for reasons other than second-hand smoke, and it is not clear how increases in information would change their position. Their rationale lies in the inconsistent preferences of cigarette smokers-- sometimes wanting to puff and sometimes wanting to kick the habit because of its unfortunate health consequences. On the other hand, there are the immediate joys foregone as a result of the ban and all sorts of deleterious consequences of the government enforcing a ban. We have seen those consequences during prohibition and the current drug scene. Weighing the favorable and unfavorable consequences of such a ban is not an easy task. But that task should be an empirical endeavor rather than part of a value assumption.

There is another difference between Friedman's position and ours. He is far more optimistic about the role of information at least in his earlier work. " Just present the information and views will change." Confirmation bias, however, makes people resistant to information if it conflicts with their policy views. Most of the information required to convert naïve altruists to informed altruists has been part of the public domain for a long time, and still naïve altruists play a crucial role in policy decisions. In their 1990 edition of Free to Choose the Friedmans conceded that they were too optimistic in their 1980 edition. Still, the only way to convert naïve altruists is through information, and, indeed, we have seen that such conversion takes place in a limited extent in the case of the minimum wage. There is even some hope that non-economic social scientists will eventually become aware of behavior that is currently unmentionable because it is not politically correct to do so. Gross (2013) notes that some younger sociologists are willing to admit that some of the problems of Blacks are attributable to pathologies associated with ghetto culture, an admission not readily made by an older generation. That is a little late given that the well-publicized Moynihan Report said the same thing in 1965. Still it is progress of a sort. The information route of Friedman is the only way to improve policy. It is just rockier than he foresaw. Information development is not enough. The dissemination of that information is no easy task.

One possible reason for the failure of increased information to achieve the kind of consensus that Friedman foresaw is the increased politicalization of universities, generating even more naïve altruists requiring converting.

CHAPTER 7

DEMOCRACY

Many philosophers believe that there is a "good" upon which all people can agree. Rawls (1990) maintained that maximizing the well-being of the least fortunate—the difference principle—was the "good". Benthamic utilitarians have assumed that there is a social utility consisting of the sum of the utility of everybody in the world, and that people of good will want to maximize this utility.

In contrast, scholars such as Haidt (2012) maintain that people differ in their innate preferences and that difference will cause them to have different views about appropriate policy even if they were all fully informed. There is, however, near universal agreement about a "fair" way of handling those differences: the democratic ideal. People can and do agree on "fair" rules of aggregating individual preferences about social rules at least in principle: give equal weight to the interests of each individual in a polity.

That is the rationale of current representative democracies, though they all have to compromise that goal because of efficiency considerations. Time costs and the unequal distribution of information rule out direct democracies in favor of representative democracies. The information problem also plagues representative democracies. Many voters are unaware of the most rudimentary features of government decisions. But the information problem also exists among people who are regarded as well informed. We have already seen how important naïve altruism is in voter decisions, an altruism based on imperfect information. Naïve altruism is an affliction most common among the well-educated.

Giving equal weight to the interests of all encompasses more than electoral rules. It also involves governmental behavior after a government is installed – "the rule of law"— equality of treatment before the law. An important component of the rule of law is "minority rights". There are often ethnic and religious differences within a polity. This sometimes means that certain groups can never be part of the majority if there is enough animosity between groups. Tranquility requires that their minority position is not devastating to their lives. In a well-functioning democracy the life opportunities of a member of a minority group should not depend on his being part of a minority.

Another component of the rule of law is "no extra privileges for people in power" –no corruption, for example. Corruption is a problem endemic to government that is probably made less severe in a democracy, especially in a democracy in which government actions are well publicized. Democracy offers the option of "throwing the rascals out" if the rascals get too greedy.

It is possible to accept the democratic ideal and still reject representative democracy in a particular case because of the myriad problems associated with the latter in that case. Some would reject a democracy that produces policy so antithetical to their views of appropriate policy. This is particularly true of the concern of others about some of the representative democracies of the Middle East.

Currently, there is widespread support for representative democracy in the Western World, where the information level of the electorate is so much greater than elsewhere. For example, with all its imperfections, there is a remarkable agreement in the United States that our current way of making decisions is appropriate. Only 4 percent of respondents to The General Social Survey of the United States for 1996 were in favor of a drastic overhaul of our government (NORC, 1996). Part of that agreement is attributable to the fact that the current way of making political decisions has been around for a long time. But the World Values Survey of many countries, including some that were not democracies, found that most people, thought that it was very important that they live in a country that was governed democratically (Achen and Bartels, 2016) And one can compare that consensus with the large amount of disagreement over any substantive policy question. Additional evidence of current support for representative democracy is the frequent effort of dictatorships to mask their dictatorships by some kind of democratic charade.

The almost universal current approval of representative democracy has made Sen (2001) declare democracy a universal value. That declaration is hard to square with the considerable disapproval of democracy in the 18th and 19th century. But these disapprovals of democracy were not attacks on the democratic ideal. Rather, they flowed from problems associated with implementing that ideal by representative democracy.

Democracy is often not popularly accepted within a polity when that polity has some other political arrangement. If the status quo is non-democratic, traditionalism motivates people to accept that non-democracy. People in power under those circumstances will also defend their power. Hence, they find as good the non-democracy that maintains their position. But these rationales of non-democracy are usually made in terms of the welfare of everybody – the democratic ideal.

Altruism has often been used in defense of democracy. Benthamic utilitarians believe that people should maximize the sum of everybody's utility, that, in that sense, one person's utility is as important as that of another. Many utilitarians accept democracy as the best practical way to achieve an approximation to maximizing social utility (Riley, 1990), since interpersonal comparisons of utility have serious difficulties which seem to require an alternative approach.

Other utilitarians propose a social welfare function (Bergson, 1938). In the social welfare function each person differentially weighs his perception of the utility of every other person and his concern with that utility by whatever weights he chooses. This then becomes his idea of what is good. The social welfare function so defined will vary by individuals. People tend to give greater weight to the well-being of their relatives and friends than they do to others. People will also vary by how altruistic they are relative to their self-interested concerns. Some kind of aggregation of individual social welfare functions is required to get to appropriate social rules.

The aggregation of individual decisions about social rules occurs in two ways. There can be some informal mechanism that determines mores. Alternatively, government can determine social rules. I focus on the latter. What would be the rules of governance that individuals would choose given enough information if they were free to choose? One of the determinants of that choice is what individuals would regard as fair rules of governance. A person's choice of fair rules of governance is determined by a combination of his wish to be considered good in that choice and his wish that his own political agenda be adopted, with the latter itself being a combination of his desires to be good and his other largely self-interested preferences.

Where do these notions of "fair" government rules come from? Conceivably, they arise as a direct results of altruism. "One person, one vote" is simply the fair way for determining government policy. But in contrast to many social ideals, the democratic ideal can be based on simple self-interest. Fairness is determined by people communicating to one another their notions of fairness. To have an effect, those notions must be acceptable to both the message giver and message recipient. But no self-interested person delivers or accepts that message unless under fairness his interests are represented by at least a proportionate share in governance within the communicating group. Since both deliverer and receiver must accept the message, in principle the interests of both must be equally represented. One expects this principle to hold for enough informed individuals so the democratic ideal is an appropriate ideal. It also is the current ideal in most of the world.

That need not describe the exact process by which near universal suffrage arises, but it has some merit even if that were the question. Excluded groups pressure current governments to become included. Without that pressure, members of the included groups would be unlikely to extend the franchise, though that convincing is made all the easier if those already voting accepted the democratic ideal.

That consent can encompass the rule of law as well. Democracy with the rule of law is more acceptable than democracy without it. The rule of law provides an insurance policy to those who might lose elections, an insurance that they can still have decent lives even if their group is an electoral loser.

All of this is based on a simple logic. Notions of fairness in rules of governance arise from agreement that a rule of government is fair. That agreement requires consent. It is no wonder that the rule of government agreed upon is a consensual rule.

On the basis of the democratic ideal there is a strong presumption in favor of representative democracy. Rulers favor themselves relative to others. The way to protect ones self-interest is to have a say in government. But the democratic ideal can prevail even when representative democracy is not present. Both Aquinas and Confucius believed that rulers should focus on the interests of the ruled. But morality rather than democracy was believed to be the hoped-for path to achieve that goal (Fukuyama, 2011).

The rationale for representative democracy via self-interest is in sharp contrast to the utilitarian rationale – democracy as a rough substitute for the unattainable maximizing of social utility. The evidence for the role of self-interest in promoting democracy is clear. There have often been restrictions on electoral eligibility, many of which are inconsistent with a utilitarian defense of democracy. Athenian slaves were not allowed to vote, and this was not because it was felt that Athenian citizens could best judge the interests of slaves. But Athenian citizens were in power and regarded it as fair that they shared this power with each other, and slaves were in no position to protest their exclusion from this power. Restrictions on the eligibility of voters have been common throughout the past history of democracies. A driving force for their removal has been protests from the excluded or a subset of the included that believed that the excluded would vote the same way they do. A case in point is the women's suffrage, largely, but not entirely, supported by women. The gradual relaxation of eligibility limits suggests that the movement toward universal suffrage was driven by the self-interest of previously excluded groups rather than altruism.

The self-interested agreement on democracy would suggest that each party to the agreement would try to interpret it in a way most favorable to them. In consequence, there are many disagreements about the details of governance. People push for rules that increase the chances that the policies they advocate will be realized: the battle over states' rights or the role of the judiciary, for example.

Conservatives push for a greater role of the states relative to the central government because that increases the chances that conservative policies will be chosen. The cost to states of redistribution is greater than the cost to national government. As economists would say, the deadweight loss to the states of any given redistributive policy is greater because the rich can move either themselves or their assets from state to state, while that option does not affect responses to national governmental policy. In consequence, states are more reluctant to engage in redistribution than the national government. States' rights, then, becomes a plank in the conservative platform.

It is not obvious how many of these disagreements over the democratic ideal can be appropriately resolved. In consequence, the democratic ideal does not generate uniquely appropriate rules of governance, or at least we do not currently know what constitutes a uniquely appropriate rule of governance. Rather, there are a range of possible solutions with no clear agreement on the particular rules. But that range does exclude certain rules of governance.

One rule of governance that on the whole promotes the preservation of democracy is dispersion of power within a democratic framework. Suppose power is sufficiently concentrated, even if that concentration is determined by elections. There is a big temptation by the person or persons in power to permanently stay in power. "One election, one person, one time." That event is more difficult to attain if many have to agree to this subversion of democracy.

Even so, it is possible sometimes to get many to agree to this subversion. The self-interested process that produces democracy tends to make people more interested in policy outcomes than in policy processes. For example, many will approve of Presidential power grabs if that power promotes the policy that they favor. Virtually the entire Hispanic community approved of President Obama's revision of immigration laws, even though such revisions would seem to be the prerogative of Congress. There is, however, some concern with procedure. There was considerable resistance to President Roosevelt's plan to expand the Supreme Court in order to have that court declare his policies constitutional, and this resistance was not confined to those who disagreed with his policy.

This simple self-interested basis for the democratic ideal is in sharp contrast to `the basis for many of the social ideals that have had a significant effect on behavior. It is consistent with aggregate self-interest while many social ideals are not.

The democratic ideal is nearly universal, though democracy is not. Its main competitor is status quo goodness in non-democratic polities, but status quo goodness is not an ideal. The same self-interest that generates an agreement that the democratic ideal is fair also generates non-democracy when consent is not required for governing. Power is often an adequate substitute for consent, a substitute that often sustains itself in a fairly long term by both the power itself and an acceptance because it is the status quo.

Primitive societies were consistently egalitarian, though often women were excluded (Boehm, 1999). In this case, nobody had the power to impose his will on group preferences and group size was small, so the democratic ideal became at least roughly the reality. When, however, group size grew larger and the power to impose one's will against others increased, democracy usually shriveled, and has only been reinvented in the modern world with an increase in education.

Altruism and the Democratic Ideal

The democratic ideal is a criterion for what constitutes good government policy--the democratically determined policy if all made their decisions with enough information and the rule of law operated. Will altruists accept the democratic ideal as their guide to good policy when others use self-interest as one of the determinants of their votes? All that we know suggests that they do accept this ideal as one of their criteria for good policy. The overwhelming support in the United States for our form of government is evidence. Just as a matter of the numbers game, many of those supporters must include altruists, naïve or otherwise. It is doubtful, however, that they would be willing to accept the democratic ideal as their sole criterion. They, like others, try to construct rules of governance that maximize the chances that their policy preferences are realized within a democratic framework. Their behavior suggests that they do not believe that the preferences of others ultimately based on the self-interest of these others should count. They make every effort consistent with a preference for democracy to make sure that those preferences do not count. They, for example, do not question Supreme Court decisions upholding their preferences even when a majority of Americans have contrary preferences. This discounting of self-interested preferences seems to be an extension of the impartiality criterion often used in philosophic discussions, that self-interest should be excluded in making moral judgements.

We have already discussed the impartiality principle: since we all have an incentive to better ourselves, that incentive affects a person's view of appropriate policy. That effect is often inconsistent with a naively altruistic view of good policy. Accordingly, they believe that self-interest should not count in determining appropriate policy for everybody. That makes sense when one is dealing with any individual. His view of what is good is biased toward his own interest. But does it make sense to demand impartiality when one is dealing with the democratic aggregation of individual preferences? That aggregation balances an individual's bias in favor of his own well-being by other individuals' biases in favor of their well-being. There is one important advantage of aggregate self-interest over altruism. It is more sharply defined. People know more about how to further their self-interest than they know about how to further the cause of altruism. There is more naïvely altruistic voting than naïve self-interested voting, not that self-interested voting always takes into account all of the consequences of policy decisions.

Probably the most famous example of the use of the impartiality principle is Rawls' "veil of ignorance" which tells people to ignore their own self-interest in determining an appropriate principle of justice. One of the problems with the veil of ignorance as a general principle is that it does not specify which characteristics a person should ignore. Should he ignore that he is not a fetus or that he is not a chimpanzee?

In Rawls' version one accepts that he is an extant human, generation unspecified. From this "veil of ignorance" Rawls then intuits his "indifference principle" where only the well-being of the poorest counts in determining an appropriate distribution of income. This is an extreme form of altruism – focus exclusively on the neediest- an extreme form that people in general reject (Froehlich et al., 1987). The reason for that rejection is that people want their own self-interest and the self-interest of others beyond the poorest to count in determining principles of justice.

If, then, we accept the democratic ideal as the appropriate way of determining appropriate policy, we must accept the views of the self-interested as well as the views of the altruists. Indeed, there is a persuasive argument that we should give greater weight to self-interested voting, an argument that we provide shortly.

Naïve altruists play lip service to the democratic ideal, but hardly practice it. They disapprove of self-interest, that is greed, determining votes just as they disapprove of it in the operation of markets except, of course, when that greed makes the greedy vote in concert with the naïve altruists. They think government policy should be determined by the "anointed" in the word used by Sowell (2009). Sowell feels they are anointed because they are members of the elite. I think they feel anointed because they think they are disinterested. Look at President Kennedy's oft-admired declaration in that light: "Ask not what your country can do for you. Rather ask what you can do for your country". But aggregate self-interest is the aggregation of people asking, "What can my country do for me?" That aggregation often produces results contrary to the preferences of naïve altruists. The latter are willing to run roughshod over those preferences to get their way. That feeling of being anointed is increased by the fact that the intellectual community is so dominated by the naïve altruists. That blessing increases their sense of righteousness.

An example of this attitude in operation is in application of the legal theory of the "living constitution." "Mores have changed from the eighteen century and the constitution must be adjusted thereby". On the basis of such adjustment, legislation prohibiting abortion should be declared unconstitutional." But, of course, the legislators who oppose abortion are responding to the mores of their constituents. But such constituent mores should not count because they are different from those of the anointed.

Similarly, many naïve altruists accept cultural relativism. "A culture can only be judged by the mores of that culture." On the basis of that doctrine they object to capitalism as practiced in the United States. The only way those positions can be made consistent is in the belief that the only mores that count are the mores of the anointed.

But let us first just look at each of the voting motivators, We can, then, ask the key question of what will happen to aggregate policy preferences as information increases. We have already provided an answer to this question for all types of voters without explicitly considering democracy. Naively altruistic voters will become less naïve and, hence, less supportive of the causes of naïve altruism. Self-interested voters will also be less supportive of these causes if they became more aware of unintended consequences with greater information. Imitation and traditions would also be less supportive of liberal causes as the population that they imitated became less supportive.

Now, let us look at the possible change in the extent of these motivators as information increased. First, look at the effect of greater information on voters motivated by tradition. With greater information there would be the realization that the traditions of free-markets and the nuclear family generate what people want. The contrary part of tradition that has been generated by the influence over time of naïve altruists would be reduced. This would reduce liberal support. On the other hand, there would be greater awareness of the increases in externalities generated by greater population density with increases in information. This should increase support for liberal environmental regulation compared to the attitude of traditionalists.

One way of determining which of these considerations actually dominates is to look at environmental regulation. The best way we have of determining whether a particular environmental law is good or bad is cost-benefit analysis, whether the costs are less than or greater than the benefits. It is conservatives, rather than liberals, that favor that criterion. In general costs are something that liberals would prefer to ignore.

The Clinton administration allowed cost-benefit analysis, but in a phony way. They included non-use benefits in their benefit calculations. We have seen earlier that that is not appropriate. Non-use benefits are the benefits of feeling good about supporting a pro- environmental rule, rather than the benefits of the rule itself.

An implication of the foregoing is that traditional cost-benefit analysis provides a lower limit estimate of the cost of public investments. Increases in information should lead people to this conclusion. Since liberals do not share that belief, greater information should make them more skeptical of public investment.

The Democratic Ideal as a Guide to Policy

That policy should become more conservative is considerably reinforced if we accept the democratic ideal as the sole criterion for good policy. That implies that altruists who are interested in good policy would accept that ideal as the basis for their altruism while non-altruists would not be affected. Democratic outcomes would then depend solely on the aggregate preferences of the non-altruists. Altruists would only prefer that those democratic outcomes be realized.

As we have seen, increases in information should increase the number of altruists. People's conversation will more likely include conversation about world affairs, and in consequence they are more likely to vote in terms of how they would like the world to behave. But even with full information people will vote to some extent in terms of their self-interest. Coal miners will talk about their current plight and vote somewhat in terms of their own interest. Self-interest is an innate preference.

With enough information self-interest voting is reduced but not to zero. On the other hand, traditional voting probably goes to zero, but so too does naïve altruism. Given the assumption that started this discussion, altruism takes the form of the democratic ideal. What is left is a combination of self-interest and the democratic ideal. But the latter simply becomes advocating aggregate self-interest. The various self-interested voting produces an aggregate self-interest. In an ideal voting process the two aggregate self-interests will be the same. But in any case some combined form of aggregate self-interest would be the outcome. I discuss in Chapter 8 the consequence of actual voting patterns diverging from those required by the democratic ideal.

The democratic ideal should have the same directional effect even if it was not considered the sole altruistic criterion. After all, as an altruistic criterion it is a substitute for alternative forms of altruism. That should increase the role of self-interest relative to naïve altruism.

But this examination of the democratic ideal in a full information world is somewhat fanciful. Voters in general have no incentive to be fully informed in their political decisions. No recommendations about information from this book or more influential sources are likely to have any impact on the behavior of the self-interested or the traditionalist. But there can be some impact on altruists, though not by demanding that they acquire more information. They can, however, get better information. There is an innate basis for altruism, but many of the specific policy views of the altruists are learned. The current education system has encouraged naïve altruism. That has resulted in not only ignoring unintended consequences, but it has not emphasized the impact of the democratic ideal on policy choices. That main impact is to give some weight to the preferences of the self-interested in determining what is good.

Both educational reforms need not increase information costs. Those emphases can be substituted for information that voters find irrelevant to their voting decisions. Of course, such reforms would not be easy to implement given the current character of colleges in particular, but it is possible to at least start.

Another problem with the democratic ideal as a guide to policy is whether it is saleable. We have seen that even people who support the democratic ideal seem to give greater weight to policy outcomes than to the process by which those outcomes are realized, even though that process can have important long-run consequences of its own. But we have also seen that sometimes process does matter. That suggests that the democratic ideal has some policy impact. Since the democratic ideal is an altruistic goal, one would expect it to be a closer substitute for other altruistic goals than for self-interested behavior. That is why we would expect emphasis on the democratic ideal to reduce the impact of naïve altruism on democratic outcomes.

Whether or not altruists accept the democratic ideal, the very existence of representative democracy should have a profound effect on sufficiently informed altruists. The purpose of the democratic ideal is to give equal weight to members of a polity. In part the poor, say, achieve that goal by voting. That partial achievement should reduce the additional redistribution to the poor that a sufficiently informed altruist would advocate.

It should be noted, however, that the use of the democratic ideal as the sole criterion for policy does not imply an acceptance of any actual representative democracy as an ideal.

The information and time requirements for direct democracy to operate in modern society are far too great, and even direct democracy would not fully satisfy the requirements of the democratic ideal. Some people are going to have more influence than others, and they will be self-interested to some extent. A representative democracy necessarily generates differences in influence, but less than virtually any other kind of governance other than a direct democracy.

Decision Making for the Decision Makers

The democratic ideal is in sharp contrast to a fairly widespread ethical ideal – inter-generational equity – held by such people as Rawls (1990), Arrow (1995) and the Catholic Church. That ideal proclaims that the interests of every future generation should be given equal weight in determining appropriate policy though future generations are not parties to current decisions. The democratic ideal proclaims that the interests of all decision makers within a polity, including their altruistic interests, should determine appropriate policy. Because people have an altruistic interest in their children, their interests will also be included in the democratic ideal. But those who favor inter-generational equity realize that current decision makers do not properly take into account the interests of future generations in terms of that equity. That is why they feel that current decision makers over-discount the future.

That concern would be appropriate if intergenerational equity would be accepted with enough information. Indeed, because of imitation, enough people asserting that intergenerational equity is good will tend to influence others in accepting that idea. But it is an idea inconsistent with innate preferences and, therefore, cannot be an ultimate winner. People innately do not give the same weight to generations far in the future that they give to themselves or their children, and there is nothing that the intergenerational equity advocates can do about that fact.

This is not a trivial issue. Many of those who propose large expenditures on global warming abatement do so in the name of intergenerational equity, for example Stern (2006). It is generally recognized by economists that the appropriate current response to global warming depends crucially on determining the appropriate rate to discount the future (See, for example, D'Arge et al., 1982). The trade-off is between current costs to reduce global warming and benefits that are primarily hundreds of years away. It is no wonder that Nordhaus and Boyer (2000) using a market discount rate get very different policy outcomes than Stern.

"Intergenerational equity" is obviously inconsistent with non-altruistic voting.

Future generations cannot vote in the present, and present voters tend to give greater weight to the present. The "intergenerational equity" folk, therefore, believe that we mistakenly underweight the long run future by a lot.

Even non-altruistic voters believe that the market somewhat underweights the future. People are, on the whole, somewhat myopic in their market behavior. There is a kind of dualism in people's preferences. There are immediate unthoughtful responses, and there are thoughtful responses that take into account the future consequences of their actions.

The alcoholic's on and off the wagon's behavior is an example of this phenomenon. But as far as a person's voting behavior is concerned, the imitation of other's self-interested behavior that counts in establishing reputation is the imitation of their voting behavior. Voting is not subject to the same temptations of immediate rewards as is market behavior because the policy returns to voting are never immediate. One expects a greater myopic difference between this year's return and next year's return than that difference between next year's return and the subsequent year's return. It is no accident that public policy tends to interfere with market choices in giving greater weight to the future. Sin taxes are the most obvious example. Of course, altruistic voting produces the same result.

It should be noted, however, that this future orientation of voting only holds when it is the predominant feature of a policy choice. Redistributive legislation often reduces payments or increases taxes as a function of a person's assets. This is a de facto tax on savings, encouraging present consumption over future consumption. However, most of the advocates of "intergenerational equity" are also advocates of greater redistribution. This is a serious intellectual conflict. Adam Smith made a point long ago, and that point has been consistently reconfirmed by the evidence: In the long run the market reduces poverty, and interferences with the market reduce this long run effect. This does not imply that the present poor cannot benefit from some redistribution, but the advocates of "intergenerational equity" are supposedly equally concerned with the long run future poor, so this long-run anti-poverty program of the market should be particularly gratifying to them, but it is not.

<u>Animal Rights</u>

Over concern with future generations is not the only problem with altruism's failure to observe the locus of policy decision-making. The bestowal of animal rights is another case. Humans make policy decisions for humans; not for chimpanzees. The reputational concerns of humans involve what other humans think of one, not what chimpanzees think. Furthermore, ones reputation among chimpanzees does not depend upon how one votes. Philosophers, such as Singer (1981), believe that the well-being of other animals should be given equal weight with the well-being of humans. This is clearly inconsistent with the self-interest of humans, and that aggregate self-interest is an essential part of the democratic ideal.

The Endangered Species act seeks what its advocates regard as environmental protection through preservation of animal (and plant) species. The noted sociobiologist Wilson (1992) proposes as a welfare criterion, "maximize the number of species." Such a criterion is inconsistent with what most people want now. Few would want to preserve the polio virus, for example. Nor would increased information change that attitude. It is in virtually no human's informed self-interest to be a polio virus supporter. In consequence, reputational goodness based on the self-interest of others would not produce polio virus advocates.

The Endangered Species Act as administered takes little account of costs. This is a general characteristic of naïve altruism, as we have seen. And costs should be considered in an appropriate altruism. That does not imply that all considerations of animal welfare should be ignored. Bird watchers require birds to be watched. Watching an animal suffer is unpleasant enough to reduce the well-being of humans. But those features of humans' preferences hardly justified most of the actions associated with the Endangered Species Act.

Social Ideals and Informed Goodness

How would policy decisions change if people were sufficiently informed? One would still expect sufficiently informed individuals to make decisions in part in terms of their self-interest and self-interested determined views of goodness. What others think and do would still affect their decisions. The big question is how social ideals would change if people were sufficiently informed.

We know that social ideals are variable. They vary culture to culture and there also is variation in the weight that people give to those ideals in determining what they think is good. Women's rights, affirmative action, environmentalism are recent manifestations of social ideals in the Western World, though compassion for the poor has to some degree or other been around for a long time.

Suppose that in the long run these ideals were completely variable. What in the long run would be the appropriate social ideals? One candidate would be the democratic ideal – an ideal that does not depend on the confirmation bias and that appears to be a fundamental part of most other ideals in operation.

Let us see what that means in terms of governmental expenditures to improve the environment. That there should be some expenditures is obvious. As most economists recognize, the market under-allocates resources to environmental expenditures because of externalities, that is, there are people who are not parties to market decisions that are affected by those decisions because of their environmental consequences. But what is the appropriate level of environmental expenditures? The beneficiaries of such expenditures as well as the tax payers are voters. Suppose nobody gets any "goodness" mileage out of advocating more environmental expenditures than is in their self-interest. Then, they and others would simply decide in terms of their self-interest and the self-interest of their groups. Then, one would get just the right amount of expenditures on these amenities in terms of some weighted average of voters' preferences. If, in addition, it is considered "good" to advocate these government expenditures, one is likely to get too much in the way of these amenities in terms of that weighted average of voter preferences. Suppose instead that people replaced the social ideal of a "good" environment with the ideal " that is good which the democratic process produces". Then, one would get just the right amount of environmental expenditures in terms of some weighted average of voters' preferences.

Whether that weighted average of voter preferences corresponds to an average consistent with the democratic ideal is another question which I am unable to answer. On the one hand, current polluters tend to have more influence in environmental regulation than do others. On the other hand, the media, educators and bureaucrats also have more influence – and they for the most part are in favor of more environmental regulation.

There is some evidence, however, that currently the pro-environment social ideal produces too great an expenditure on the environment. It is the pro-environmental advocates that reject the use of cost-benefit analysis in determining the levels of environmental expenditures, for example, the EPA's interpretation of the Clean Air Act. The contrast between the EPA's interpretation and the Supreme Court's rejection of that interpretation is instructive. The EPA has taken the view of the naïve altruist, while the Supreme Court has plunked for a cost-benefit approach.

Cost-benefit analysis comes reasonably close to an aggregation of voter preferences consistent with the democratic ideal. On the benefit ledger each person's benefit in terms of mortality or morbidity is weighted equally. On the cost side given our tax system any increase in expenditures hurts the rich more than it does the poor. But the rich are not on that account more opposed to environmental expenditures than the poor (Inglehart et. al, 1998) in part because the rich value a cleaner environment more than do the poor sufficiently to pay the higher taxes implied by government action to produce a cleaner environment.

Perhaps the most glaring manifestation of this over emphasis on the environment occurs in the use of "non-use values" in determining economic policy. In surveys – and one presumes in their voting behavior – people are willing to pay considerably for environmental amenities that they or their progeny will never use. Many environmental economists try to rationalize this behavior by saying that these non-users are being altruistic toward users of the amenity. Milgrom (1993) has a particularly telling point about this particular use of altruism. Why should non-users be more altruistic toward users than users are toward non-users? Why don't users altruistically take into account the interests of non-users who have to pay their share of the taxes for the amenity they do not want? After all, the stereotypical bird watcher is not noted for her selfishness. The obvious explanation for non-use values is that it is "good" to be green. Under Clinton, it was proclaimed that these non-use values should be considered in determining the benefits of environmental policy. But this leads to greater expenditures on environmental amenities than would be produced by considering simply people's preferences as assessed by their use value for these amenities.

The foregoing analysis was based on the assumption that social ideals in the long run are sufficiently variable to include the social ideal: " whatever the democratic ideal produces without the other ideals is right". A strong case can be made for that assumption in the case of environmental expenditures. Environmentalism is a recent phenomenon in the Western World. People care about environmental amenities just as they care for other goods and services, and there have been efforts in the past to reduce the health cost of sewage and other environmental efforts. But environmentalism as a belief that the environment has a value in addition to any human centered value is of recent vintage and does not correspond to any innate preference possessed by man.

The contention that the environmental ideal would disappear with additional information is supported by our previous hypothesis about the origins of many ideals – that untoward consequences of these ideals are downplayed because of the confirmation bias. Those with enough information would properly weigh the unfortunate consequences of environmental legislation together with the fortunate consequences.

Ideals vs. Aggregate Self-Interest

There has to be some explanation for the inconsistency of many ideals and aggregate self-interest. In the case of the environmental ideal I know of only one alternative hypothesis. Singer (1981) believes that in the process of convincing others to take his interests into account, a person must proclaim positions that take the interests of others into account as well as his own. A person, then, begins to believe in those positions. Singer believes that these generalized interest positions tend to get broader and broader over time until they incorporate the whole of the animal kingdom. Singer's position about how agreement among people can occur is approximately correct. He is also correct in surmising that on the whole people's positions have become less parochial over time. The big problem with Singer, however, is why the need for agreement among others makes people advocate animal rights. Agreement among all animals is neither required to produce the agreement required for groups of humans to make decisions, nor is such agreement possible. Other animals are not part of the human decision process.

The Democratic Ideal and Utilitarianism

But can one get to the democratic ideal or at least move toward such an ideal given the current dominance of other, dramatically different, ideals? The closest extant ideal to that I propose is utilitarianism. This is a form of utilitarianism that considers only human wellbeing. That utilitarianism is inconsistent with the extreme forms of environmentalism and the Rawls' difference principle as far as issues of redistribution are concerned. Otherwise, contrary to many of its advocates, utilitarianism has little to say about redistribution. (Most of the redistributive implications of utilitarianism require the contrary to fact assumption that people with different incomes are the same except for their differences in income.)

The big difference between utilitarianism and the democratic ideal is that utilitarianism proposes to aggregate individual well-being by their utility and the democratic ideal aggregates individual wellbeing by their vote. This leads to another difference between the democratic ideal and utilitarianism. The latter asserts the doctrine of consumer sovereignty as a value. Whatever consumers choose with enough information is good, taking into account the impact of externalities. The democratic ideal proclaims that what voters choose with enough information is good. Accepting the latter value means that if there is a conflict between what an informed voter wants and what an informed consumer wants, the former is the appropriate guide.

However, in most cases at the present level of both voter and market information, the democratic ideal is likely to lead to similar results as utilitarianism because market players know so much more about the crucial determinants of their decisions than do voters. It pays them to know more in their market role than in their voter role and that difference usually extends to the bureaucrats that voters very indirectly select. That is the theme of much of the work of Hayek (1994).

Utilitarianism and Myopia

But there is a different difference between informed voters and informed consumers that prevails in our world of less than perfect information. Voter myopia is not as great as consumer myopia. Even fully informed consumers tend to give less weight to the future than they would as voters. Consumer decisions are based in part on immediate wants and in part on a thoughtful consideration of present and future consequences: for example, a consumer who tries to quit smoking cigarettes on the basis of his thoughtful evaluation of their consequences, but who has only indifferent success. In contrast, the consequences of votes are delayed so that immediate wants play a lesser role. Sin taxes, sometimes assessed when the majority sin, are the most obvious example of this difference in behavior.

Frederick et al. (2002) summarized the research on time discounting. One study showed that as far as individual preferences were concerned there was a one month discount rate of 360% compared to a 19% discount rate over a ten year time horizon. This is evidence for bodily time preference of the immediate compared to thoughtful time preferences.

Curiously enough, however, government policy on the whole discourages savings even though an increase in savings is one of the main consequences of people discounting the future less. This peculiarity of government policy is because greater concern with the future has been given less weight than other motivations, in particular the interest in redistribution. Means testing as part of government policy nearly always uses an asset ceiling to determine eligibility. This discourages savings. But the biggest culprit has been Social Security in most countries which pays currently out of receipts gathered currently and thus creates no social savings. At the same time its presence discourages individuals from saving for retirement. This was all designed to create political support for Social Security from the aged at the time of the initial passage of Social Security.

"Intergenerational equity" is obviously inconsistent with non-altruistic voting. Future generations cannot vote in the present, and present voters tend to give greater weight to the present. The "intergenerational equity" folk, therefore, believe that we mistakenly underweight the long run future by a lot.

Nations

Simple altruism does not explain a feature of democracy -- the co-existence of multiple nation states. We do not have a world government, or even a government that encompasses all of the Western World. World government is not what one would expect from a self-interested development of democracy. People are afraid of what such a government would do to their cultural values and rich countries are afraid of the redistribution of their wealth that might occur if they were joined hand and foot to a poorer country with a "one person, one vote" principle.

One way to agree in the face of disagreement about how to get together is to agree to go one's own way. That independence does not imply isolation. Nations can construct treaties with one another, treaties enforced by a combination of direct self-interest, reciprocity, and reputational damage from breaking treaties. Sometimes, of course, that enforcement machinery is not enough to prevent disastrous interactions. But it is clear that agreement on a common government did not occur, and its failure to occur could not be attributable to lack of information. The possibility of wars is not something that has recently occurred to us.

There is another important advantage of multiple national states – an informational advantage. People can compare the outcomes of different social systems in operation in determining which social system they want. Would people have so readily realized that there was something fundamentally flawed in Eastern European economies prior to the lifting of the Iron Curtain if they had not seen how much better the West was doing? The information gleaned from cross country comparisons is better than time series information – comparisons of how much better off one is during one political party's tenure than before, say. The latter comparison fails to capture many of the long run consequences of economic policy, which tend to be very important.

The message that I want to emphasize is the dominance of the informed agreement principle over altruism in terms of actual behavior, behavior that is not simply produced by lack of information. People who regard themselves as committed democrats accept as a matter of course many deviations from an altruistically based democracy. However, that is not the way many philosophers try to determine the "social good." In my view such attempts have been arbitrary. They are disconnected from what people prefer now and would prefer if they had more information.

Examine the thought experiment closely related to the multiple nation problem. Suppose a world composed entirely of Robinson Crusoes, each on their deserted islands and with no man Friday. Then, we would not have to consider "the social good" at all. In spite of the fact that there are many such Crusoes, there is no need for agreement, so no need to determine what informed agreement would look like.

One gets a similar result for multiple nation states. Constrained by assorted treaty and reciprocity obligations, and as far as simple self-interest is concerned, rules for agreement within a nation state would not consider the well-being of people outside the state except for their indirect effects on the well-being of people within the state. In fact, assorted social interactions with others will by the process of imitation generate some concern. In particular, notions of fairness within a country are influenced by what people outside a country think. But the focus of national concern will still be on the interests of a state's own citizens and that focus will remain with additional information. No summing up the utilities of everybody in the world to get appropriate social rules for policy within a state. Decision-makers are interested primarily in their own well-being.

Why does this nation state agreement to go your own way not occur within a state? Why is there no agreement that individuals can opt out of both state services and taxes if they so choose? One of the same motivations would seem to apply equally to both cases. A wealthy nation would be worried about redistribution if it were to join a world government. Many wealthy persons are unhappy about the redistributive consequences of the polity of which they are a part. However, there are at least two differences between the two cases. First of all, a wealthy nation has enough power to sustain its independence if it so chooses. A wealthy person is in no such position if others in the society do not agree to allow him to be an independent entity.

Secondly, a rich person is unlikely to choose independence even if that were an option. We are all too interdependent for that. The state has monopoly power over a variety of services. Some of these services seem intrinsic to the operation of government: the court system, for example. Some of these services could be privatized, but because of economies of scale monopoly power would still tend to exist. Since these services are so vital, any independent person needs them. The state, then, can dictate a price schedule for those services that creates the redistribution that the rich had tried to avoid by being independent. This time, however, the redistribution is likely to be greater because the rich no longer have a say in what the government does. That individual independence within a society has never existed suggests that it is not a feasible option. There is no reason to suspect that it would become more feasible with greater information.

<u>Conclusion</u>

To determine appropriate policy it is helpful to have appropriate policy goals. I start with the values tautology: people would want what they would choose if they had enough information. Their desires are constrained by their innate preferences. But there is often a clash between innate preferences— especially the self-interested preference versus empathy. The desired policy is how that clash would be resolved if the members of the polity had enough information. Currently, many of the empathetic are naïve altruists, naïve in the sense that they ignore the unintended consequences of their empathy. Those unintended consequences consistently make the empathetic advocate more than an optimal amount of these interventions. As a result, many naïve altruists would become less supportive of those government interventions if they were better informed.

But it is likely that even with enough information people will disagree about appropriate policy. To determine what social rules people want it is necessary to aggregate those preferences. The best way of doing so is to give equal weight to each individual in the polity if they were sufficiently informed. This constitutes the democratic ideal. This is the kind of aggregation upon which people could agree. Representative democracy with the rule of law seems to be the best imperfect approximation of the democratic ideal available. It arose primarily by non-franchised groups demanding that they be franchised and having enough clout to make their demands a reality.

Most altruists accept the democratic ideal as a criterion for good policy at least in principle. However, many of these naïve altruists do not find the preferences of those who disagree with them worthy of consideration. Using an all-inclusive notion of democracy, information should generate a demand for less government interferences with the market than is occurring currently. Information about unintended consequences would reduce the support for those interferences from the previously naïve altruists. Democracy also implies that the beneficiaries of altruistic concern would vote their own concerns, requiring less altruistic intervention on their behalf.

More interestingly, to the extent that altruists use the democratic ideal as their criterion for the good society, they take into account the aggregated self-interested concerns of the electorate. That will increase the impact of that criterion in determining policy, and, in consequence, increase the role of conservatives in government.

CHAPTER 8

EXAMINING LIBERAL IDEAS

The Rich Have Too Much Power

One of the standard liberal complaints about representative democracy is that the rich have undue influence on government policy. There is some empirical support for such a proposition. Benjamin and Gillins (2014) relate congressional decisions on the declared positions of average citizens, rich citizens, and interest groups. They find that the latter two have a positive effect, but the first does not. They feel that it is perfectly obvious why the wealthy should have this impact on congressional action. And, indeed, a rich person through campaign contributions and greater influence in general has more political clout than a poor person. This has lead people such as Stiglitz (2012) and Achen and Baretels (2016) to maintain that the rich as a class benefit more than the poor in our democracy.

However, this case runs counter to another obvious fact. In virtually all representative democracies government sponsored redistribution is from rich to poor. There are both progressive taxes and a wide variety of programs to help the poor.

One explanation for this redistribution to the poor is altruism. The rich are more altruistic than the poor because they discuss more among themselves how the world behaves than the poor. More importantly, current altruism is in favor of redistribution to the poor. The altruistic poor are not in favor of less to the poor.

But there is also an underlying self-interested reason for redistribution from rich to poor. A rich person's vote is less responsive to a per capita dollar change in income for the rich as a class by way of government action than the response of others to that change in their income. That voting response parallels a standard view about the rich's consumption—that a dollar increase in their income generates less joy than it does to others. By itself this voting preference would make it pay politically for politicians to redistribute dollars from the rich to others. Also, the rich's influence on government is not as focused on helping the rich as a class. The magnitude of other fish to fry is greater for them than it is for the poor.

How does one reconcile the Benjamin and Gillins' evidence and the obvious character of redistribution? Benjamin and Gillins make no attempt to differentiate congressional decisions by the magnitude of their impact on group self-interest, though the issues involved in their study must be important enough to interest pollsters. But their large sample size would suggest that most of the issues examined were not of special interest to the general electorate, and many that were were about cultural rather than economic issues. A predominant number of issues dominated by the wealthy is consistent with their minor influence on redistribution by income classes.

It is generally recognized that the Republican Party's policies are more favorable to the rich as a class than the Democratic Party's. The most obvious way the rich could serve the interests of the rich as a class is to support the Republican Party in a way that the rich can be uniquely effective— campaign contributions. Yet Bonica et al. (2013) report that the political contributions of the richest one percent are roughly equally distributed between the Democratic and Republican parties. Since the mid-1990's there were six election periods where the Democrats raised more from this group and four election periods where the Republicans were the winners for this group. Contrary to the general view, their explanation for this phenomenon is that both parties are interested in protecting the rich and that is why politicians have done virtually nothing to resist the growing income inequality.

That explanation does not hold water. For the most part the growing income inequality is a product of technological change that has increased the relative demand for more highly educated workers. Government has increased that impact through the low interest regimen of the Federal Reserve that increased the value of assets. But this was an anti-recession move rather than a move to favor the rich.

Government redistributive expenditures have increased considerably over time mostly under the aegis of the Democratic Party -- Medicare, Medicaid, Obamacare, the expansion of food stamps and unemployment compensation, etc. Not only that. The Democratic Party has identified itself publicly as the anti-rich party. But that has not prevented higher income groups from contributing to the Democratic Party as much as they have contributed to Republicans.

Not only do the rich as individuals spread their contributions equally between the two political parties. The wealthier own more than their proportionate share of corporations. Total corporate political expenditures are also approximately equally distributed between the two political parties, though some individual corporations do specialize in contributing to only one party.

That does not imply that the campaign contributions of corporations and the rich do not affect policy. The implication is only that it has little effect on redistribution to the rich as a class. Corporate welfare can be generated by these contributions, and that produces serious problems of its own.

Some of the contributions of the rich against the self-interest of the rich in general is motivated by their own special interests, just like corporations. For example, rich lawyers have an incentive to contribute to Democrats, who are friendly to lawyerly interests. However, unless a party specializes in a particular special interest, these interest groups have an incentive to protect themselves by giving to both parties. But each member of the richest one percent tend to specialize in one of the parties (Bonica et al., 2013), suggesting a lot of party specialization by interest group and ideological specialization by rich individuals. In summary, the rich do not do a very good job in protecting the interests of the rich as a class.

The most important groups with influence greater than their share of the electorate are educators, the media, the bureaucracy, and elected government officials. Like the rich, they do not use those shares dominantly to protect the interest of their groups. But they have characteristics that systematically influence elections. At present, the first three have a greater proportion of naïve altruists than voters in general. To the extent that elected government officials respond to voter preferences, elected officials on average would reflect those preferences on average. But elected officials are also influenced by their own preferences. Those preferences are influenced somewhat more by educators' preferences than the population as a whole, since a greater than average proportion of these officials are college educated. That would imply that current naive altruists have more influence in extant representative democracies than they would in the democratic ideal. This is another reason to advocate policies in the direction produced by aggregate self-interest, as far as such issues as income redistribution and the environment are concerned.

That college educators have more influence than would be appropriate in terms of the democratic ideal is usually overlooked. After all, they have only a marginal self-interest in most policy questions, so their greater influence would appear to be benign: the influence of greater information rather than lining their own nests. But we have seen that the naïve altruism that motivates most college professors is not the product of greater information. On the contrary it does, indeed, create a bias contrary to the democratic ideal even though it is not a bias produced by their self-interest.

Special Interests

There is another important difference between representative democracies and the democratic ideal – special interests. Special interests are minority groups that have more than a proportionate share of influence on some policy decision of special interest to that group. Though democracies depend on majority votes, minorities can have a disproportionate influence on public policy about their issues by concentrating their attention on those issues.

A necessary condition for an outsized influence of a minority group is that it gains more per capita than the majority loses per capita. Money transfers are the most obvious example. That difference will tend to make individual minority members more concerned about their issue than are members of the majority.

That tendency has to counter economies of scale in the distribution of information. Suppose we are dealing with a media that is not specialized in reaching a particular interest group. Then the cost per capita of relevant information through that media will be higher for members of the interest group than for the majority. Specialized media go a long way toward countering this disadvantage. That specialized media still might be more expensive per capita than non-specialized media, but the specialized media can provide non-political as well as political information. In consequence, members of the interest group might be willing to pay a higher price for the combined information.

If the interest group is small enough, the returns per member of an individual's political actions might be great enough to warrant his acquiring the political information irrespective of other returns from reading the specialized media. But often the interest group is too large to overcome the free rider problem, cotton farmers for example. In that case political information to that interest group works because it is associated with other information of interest to that group. When a minority group can be so organized, it can succeed in getting special favors in spite of the costs that benefit no one usually associated with these favors. Assorted tax loopholes are the standard example. Tax favors for a particular business cause it to use more resources than market forces would have it do. In consequence, those additional resources could be better used elsewhere.

The only way to partially counter these assaults on the democratic ideal is to make these transfers to minority groups sufficiently important to the majority that they can be reduced. A way of doing so is to make the legislation so broad that it affects the majority sufficiently that they are willing to stop it – tax reform proposals associated with general reductions in loopholes, for example. Another less likely way to increase majority information about any particular issue is to reduce the number of issues that the majority faces in voting. The simpler the government the more likely people in general will be informed about how government operates. That point has been made by Somin (2013).

A very strong case can be made for the importance of the majority's lack of information in generating the power of special interests. Becker (1983) provided the basis for this case, even though he was arguing strongly against it. The Chicago School, of which he was a part, believed that for all practical purposes political decisions are made as if there were perfect information for those making those decisions. An implication of that position is that the political system produces an optimal redistribution of income, given the organizational power of the groups vying for additional income.

One of the big costs of redistribution is deadweight loss. Except when there is a case of market failure, changing the market distribution of income by government results in less total income because incentives get distorted. A perfectly informed electorate would make deals between groups such that that deadweight loss would be minimized, since that would enable both minority and majority to get more than they would otherwise receive. Becker emphasizes this implication of his analysis, but that is the very invalidity that destroys the perfect information assumption on which it is based.

From agricultural subsidies to tariffs, economists have found large deadweight losses associated with special interest legislation. These large losses are consistent with perfect information only if there were no alternative way of redistributing to the minority that generated smaller deadweight losses. But there would appear to be an alternative: lump sum payments to the present members of the winning minority equivalent to what the majority would lose from the market distorting legislation in the minority's favor. (Such a payment eliminates some of the usual deadweight loss, but it does not prevent the resource expenditures of the minority and others over the division of the spoils.)

Becker could argue in rebuttal that the beneficiaries of the lump sum payments are not quite the same as the beneficiaries of the market distorting legislation. The latter would also include entrants to the industry attracted by its new found wealth. However, potential entrants should have less political clout than people already in the industry. Many potential entrants do not know in advance of the legislation that they will become actual entrants. Nor is their expected gain as great per person because on the whole they have better alternative options than those currently in the industry. Restricting beneficiaries to those already in the industry must, therefore, be an arrangement preferred by a coalition that would be more effective than the coalition including potential entrants. The majority would by the same token be indifferent, since the costs to them of the two arrangements would be the same.

There is a very good reason why such lump sum payments to the minority are rarely observed. The lump sum payments are too obviously what they are – payoffs to the minority at the expense of the majority. Suppose such payments cannot be rationalized as having external benefits to the majority or as acts of "goodness". Then, these lump sum payments will generate more opposition from the majority than is produced by requiring the minority to do something for their gain. That something might, indeed, generate worse impacts than if the minority did nothing at all. However, as long as a majority of the majority believes the contrary, the less efficient, less blatant transfer to the minority will prevail. For example, a building contractor friend of a politician is usually required to build a building, perhaps at an inflated price and perhaps with shoddy building materials. He cannot simply walk off with a gift at public expense, though that gift might very well have been the better alternative for the polity. Indeed, special interests do use considerable resources to convince that part of the majority that is aware of their efforts that those efforts are in the public good, for example, their specious defense of tariffs.

That there can be a return to being a member of a well-organized minority group seems to be inconsistent with conflict focused on efforts to become+ a majority group. One of the reasons for that apparent inconsistency is that there can be political returns that are not simply money transfers. The choice of national language or state religion, for example, is the same per capita return to a majority member as to a minority member. There can also be such intense differences between a majority coalition and a minority coalition that the latter are never allowed to be members of a winning political group.

This discussion of special interests indicates situations where the simple aggregation of self-interest in a representative democracy leads to results inconsistent with those that would be achieved under the democratic ideal. But that would not seem to be corrected by government action that is not focused on those special situations. That corporate welfare is a serious problem hardly justifies higher taxes on the rich than would otherwise be appropriate, even though some of the rich are gainers from special interest legislation. Many rich are not beneficiaries of corporate welfare and many non-rich are beneficiaries of special interest legislation. Take the dairy industry for example . Furthermore, taxing the rich does not correct one of the greatest defects of the role of special interest, wasting resources that could be better spent.

The Indirect Effects of Increases in Income

Some liberals have a counter argument to my policy position. They focus on the externalities associated with increases in income. They claim that these externalities are quite different for different levels of income. At lower levels of income other people gain when an individual increases his income. Crime diminishes and quality of children go up at least where the increase in individual's income increase is generated by his own efforts. That qualifying clause is often ignored. What produces the positive externality is not income per se, but the individual characteristics that tend to produce that higher income. The best evidence for that is the fate of many initially low income migrant groups contrasted with the Black ghetto.

At higher levels of income liberals claim that there are negative externalities. The process on which they focus is the status market. One man's increase in status associated with an increase in income means that somebody else's status is reduced. Status is a zero-sum game, such people as Frank (1999) maintain.

This purported negative externality at higher levels of income together with the positive externalities at lower levels of income supports two policy preferences of liberals. They want more redistribution, though the rationale for positive externalities at lower levels of income is much less persuasive when that increase in income is produced by government handouts Does the quality of children go up and the crime rate go down with increases in welfare payments?

Liberals also want more public investment financed by taxing the rich. Economists' standard way of evaluating public investment is to compare the benefits of that investment with the cost in private income foregone. But if part of that private income is used by consumers to increase their status, that part should not be counted as a cost to public investment if status is a zero-sum game.

In contrast to private income, a public investment has no status return so does not affect the measure of its benefits. Frank argues that this means that traditional cost-benefit analysis overstates the cost of public investment, while not affecting its benefits. In consequence, that analysis could reject a public investment that should have been accepted.

But what is this thing called status? Where status is not conferred by government with its grant of attendant power, ones status rank is determined by the favorable or unfavorable opinion of others and what that does to ones opinion of oneself. So defined, status is a much broader phenomenon than the focus of the status literature.

One of the most important determinants of a person's status is what others think about his trustworthiness. In non-status contexts the literature talks a lot about the importance of trust. Many useful interactions between people require trust. The timing of gains and costs often are different for different people in these interactions. Those who gain later must trust the earlier gainers to fulfill the earlier gainers' obligations. Enforceable contracts help achieve this goal, but they can go only so far given the wide variety of unforeseen circumstances that could occur. Trustworthiness helps in insuring that nobody tries to wiggle out of their contractual obligations, and trust is important in enabling implicit contracts to work. It is not surprising then that economists have found that greater trust in a unit produces greater economic growth. For example, Algan and Cahuc, 2010. Reciprocal relationships are only viable in an atmosphere of trust.

The literature also finds that people are more trustworthy the higher their income, that is, a person is more likely to be trustworthy to people in general the higher his income, for example, Kazemipur, 2006. Trustworthiness is also a function of similarity. One is more likely to trust a would-be associate than somebody else. But this kind of trust is overall not a monotonic function of income. Rather, it is ones average trustworthiness to others – a generalized trustworthiness - that is our concern.

Self-interest produces the relationship between generalized trust and income. It pays people to be more concerned with their reputation the higher their income. The returns to a good reputation are future returns. The higher ones income, the more weight he gives to the future compared with the present. With higher income he needs to borrow less for future consumption, and borrowing costs are greater than lending costs.

Credit markets operate on that principle if for no other reason than the simple fact that a person with more money is more likely to pay any given debt. But the relationship between income and trustworthiness goes more deeply than that. The higher their income, the more people are willing to pay to be good in a manner that they and others can agree constitutes "goodness". (In economist's lingo goodness has a positive income elasticity.) For example, the probability of voting increases with income even when one controls for education (Nelson and Greene, 2003). The dominant motivation for voting is the view that that is required of a good citizen. Trustworthiness is also an agreed part of being good.

Trust by itself produces a positive externality of income. Take first the simple case where any two people can form a relationship where trust is important, and a person does not capture all of the returns for being trustworthy. The latter condition is satisfied in practice because people seek out the most trusty in their relationships, which they would not do if the more trusty got all the gains from that condition. Then everybody gains from somebody becoming more trustworthy because of an increase in his income. There is more trust to be shared.

But let us look at a trust case more like the standard status case. Suppose people in one group are restricted in their relationships to somebody in another group. For example, there could be a complementarity in skills that define the relationship. Suppose further, that each person in either group seek out the most trustworthy that they can get in the other group. Then, an increase in trustworthiness produced by a person's increase in income allows him to get a trustier person in the other group. But this, then, reduces the availability of more trusty people for other members of his group.

One could argue the trust case in the same way that Frank argues his status case. A person often wants to deal with the most trustworthy person he can. But that latter person can be shut out of the deal if somebody comes along who is even more trustworthy. This produces a negative externality of the income increase that has made the interloper trustier.

What's wrong with that argument? There are two sides of this trust market: the group to which the person with the higher income belongs, a competitor's side. But there are the members of the other group. The latter gain from an increase in trust on the other side, the consumer side. As shown in the Appendix, the consumer returns are far greater than the expected competitor's losses. Consumers gain more from trusty partners than the competitors lose because on net there is more trust to share. There is unanimous agreement in the literature on the social benefits of greater deserved trust.

The trust literature is not alone in rightly ignoring competitor's cost. The same two sided argument is relevant to markets in general. An innovation that reduces prices or improves quality costs competitors, some of whose costs are sunk costs. But that innovation increases the returns to consumers, since the innovator cannot capture all of the returns himself. That latter effect is so much more important than the effect on competitors.

Just as in the trust literature, the status literature ignores one side of the market, but this time they ignore the consumer side. Probably the most important status concerns of an individual occur in voluntary associations: friendships and marriage. Since these relationships are voluntary, people do not enter into these relationships unless they gain by so doing. This hold true for both the higher and the lower status person. As demonstrated in the Appendix, voluntary associations produce positive externalities from status. The Appendix also looks at another feature of the status market analyzed by Becker et al. (2005). This also does not produce the usual negative externalities associated with status.

This examination of status assumes that the lower status person has chosen an association with a higher status person so must be getting something out of that association. It is possible that the lower status person gets nothing out of the arrangement that produces some psychological damage to him. This is the case generally assumed in the literature, and this too could operate.

But what happens in the case of status is not the crucial issue. It is, "Whether in total there are positive or negative externalities associated with higher income?" There are a lot of processes at work other than simply status. It is the answer to that broader question as far as income groups are concerned that generates more or less support for both income redistribution and public investment.

Higher income areas provide better opportunities for a worker when he changes jobs. If the land is paved with gold, there is some chance that any person or his progeny can share in that gold. That chance yields a positive externality from any individual's increase in wages. That increase can potentially be shared by others.

There are more sources of positive externalities of income. Higher incomes encourage risk-taking because the rich are greater risk-takers. This encouragement occurs both because the funds available for risk-taking are greater with higher incomes and the incentive to engage in risky activities are increased (Conard, 2012). Some of the greatest risk-takers are entrepreneurs and innovators. Both activities yield social returns greater than their private returns, since they produce a consumer surplus, as we have seen.

Another external benefit of higher private income is generated through the tax system. Government revenues plunge when private incomes decline with recessions, for example. Even with proportional taxes, the rich pay more in taxes than the poor. For any given tax structure, greater private income generates greater public amenities financed via taxes. With progressive taxes this externality is even more important for taxing higher income groups.

Charity has similar effects. There is some social benefit to most charities or they would not exist. Charity increases with income and, hence, provides an external benefit to those increases.

Increased income also has external returns on the consumption side. Innovation frequently produces initially expensive products that only the rich can afford. Later, with more innovation and scale economies, versions of these products become less expensive so have a mass market. But many of these products would not have gotten started if it had it not been the existence of the rich as initial consumers.

The rich also provide a market for the amenities that the rich prefer—the theater, art museums, fancy restaurants, and so forth. While these are an externality not for everybody, these are externalities for the well to do, an externality not connected to any associations that we have previously discussed. These amenities do not in any substantial way prevent the availability of amenities for the less well-off. There are so many more of the amenities for those groups that a slight decline in the market for them produces no real negative externalities.

All in all and considering status as well, it would appear that there are positive externalities associated with increases in income even at the upper end of the income distribution.

The liberal argument for more redistribution and greater public investment on account of income externalities requires another assumption –that these externalities are not well known to voters. Otherwise they would have been taken into account by voters already, and, hence, already have affected policy outcomes. I believe that assumption to be correct. But if income externalities are positive on the whole, that assumption leads to just the opposite conclusions that some liberals are pushing.

APPENDIX

STATUS

Instead of looking at trust in this Appendix, I look at an almost identical case of the operation of status in the case of voluntary associations. (The words change somewhat but the analysis is the same.) Voluntary associations produce a positive externality to increases in income through the status market. The simplest case to analyze is the case of monogamous marriage. This process of matching is associated with a two-sided return to status, a male and a female return. Both males and females vary within groups in what they have to offer to each other. In the simplest case the variable is the joint income after marriage. The analysis is the same when parts of what one party wants after marriage are characteristics of the other, say pulchritude. All we have to do is consider the income equivalent of those characteristics. Then, suppose some male, say male 1, increases his income and so can increase his contribution to the joint income after marriage or its equivalent. This increases his desirability and so he can marry a higher income female. As a consequence, the other males have to be satisfied with lower income females. That produces a negative externality. But females are on average going to be better off. It turns out that females are better off more than the males other than male 1 are worse off in terms of income. There is a simple reason for this phenomenon. The total joint income shared by everybody other than male 1 has gone up because male 1 shares his income after marriage and his income has gone up. On net, there is a positive externality.

But we have not considered any psychological benefits or costs associated with status. People might get some pleasure to being kowtowed to and kowtowing can be unpleasant. What role one plays in this kowtowing depends upon whether one contributes more or less to the joint income after marriage. These psychological costs and benefits do behave as in the traditional view of status given the assumption that the deference relationship depends on the difference between the contributions of each party to the joint after marriage income. By itself the deference relationship tends to produce a negative externality. Since male 1 gains in kowtowing , the net of the kowtowing process for everybody else must be negative.

Crucially, though, both the psychological costs and benefits have to be less than the returns from trying to choose a higher income person or neither males or females would make such choices. I assume the simplest relationship where both the costs of kowtowing and the returns to being kowtowed to are directly proportional to the difference between the parties contribution to joint income after marriage but in both cases the crucial coefficient is less than 1   That implies that the direct payoff in joint income to others than male 1 will be greater than their net kowtowing costs. He has added both greater joint income for others and their net kowtowing costs, but the latter must be smaller than the former. There will still be a positive externality as before, but it will be somewhat less.

Status considerations in voluntary associations have another virtue. In a perfect information world dominated by self-interest considerations, a person would properly take into account the greater joint income that he would have in addition to his own income because of shared income after marriage. But he would not take into account the greater shared income of the other party. In consequence, from the point of view of society, he undervalues that shared income. Receiving a status return provides him an incentive to both increase the joint return beyond his own share of that return. That will encourage him both to work harder and to choose those features of his consumption that generate greater joint income.

One can analyze voluntary associations of any kind in the same way as we looked at marriage. People on the whole prefer to associate with a higher income person. The amenities are better, the business contacts are likely to be more useful, the friends one is likely to meet are also more likely to be interesting, since richer people can afford to be more selective precisely because others want their association. For those reasons a higher income person gets a status return in the relationship with a lower income person supposing that their other characteristics are equally attractive.

Just as in the marriage case, we can look at the friendship case as a two-sided affair. But in the friendship case every person wears two hats. All are competitors and all are recipients of the largesse of each other. We can, then, analyze the friendship model just like the marriage model by looking at both roles separately. The competitor role will be just like the male role in the case of an increase in income of a male. The recipient of some part of the income of friends then plays the female role. Then, the monogamous marriage analysis remains essentially unchanged in the case of only one friend, and its extension to many friends only complicates the analysis without changing its results. Again, because of sharing there will be more income for others to share, and, hence, a positive externality. Psychological status considerations generates a negative externality, but not enough to prevent a net positive externality.

How about jobs that involve contact with the boss? With job alternatives there is again a voluntary association. The employee's kowtowing must be valued less than his gain in his present job compared to his next best alternative. With a perfectly competitive labor market that gain is 0, so no kowtowing. However, given search costs, there can be some, but limited kowtowing. Also, to minimize turnover, the firm has an incentive to keep the kowtowing at a minimum. Furthermore, this status game is not connected to the boss's income. It is the boss's status as boss qua boss rather than his income that counts.

But the workplace also requires some association with fellow employees. But in this case the status relationships are dominated by either seniority or competence, neither of which are generated by higher income, though they can generate higher income.

It is possible that status concerns can occur in the absence of any association or in involuntary associations. One can envy Bill Gates and conceivably that reduces one's happiness, though no kowtowing is required in this case. Certainly, the cry of "inequality" is a frequent political theme and it must work to some degree or it would not be employed. However, it is not clear that inequality concern is generated by the simple desire to have more oneself or some underlying envy. That people flock to the houses of the rich when they can, suggests that the envy thus generated is less than the pleasure they get from seeing those houses. This envy about circumstances that do not affect one's life could produce negative externalities to increases in income.

This envy is likely to be largely culturally determined-people for political gain telling others that they ought to be envious, Envy is not simply determined by income inequality. There are at least two strikes against envy advocacy from our point of view. The policies proposed by its advocates are unfortunate and greater envy by itself is a cause of unhappiness. Even with the existence of envy, I suspect that the negative externalities thus generated do not dominate the positive externalities associated with the relationships that do affect one's life.

Becker et al. (2005) provided a quite different rationale for a positive externality associated with status. Under what I regard as quite special conditions the status market creates risky behavior which in turn generates social benefits. The most important conditions are a status good in fixed supply that is different than income and higher status individuals getting greater marginal value out of additional consumption. It is not clear what happens when those assumptions are relaxed.

APPENDIX

UNINTENDED CONSEQUENCES

Suppose that prior to the unintended consequences of a government action there is an equal chance that a product is being over or under produced by the same amount compared to the true competitive ideal. In both cases assume that there is a market interference that increases the output of that product by the same amount. The expected magnitude of the deviation from the competitive ideal will be greater after the interference than before. The interference toward the competitive ideal can overshoot, that is, more than correct the previous deviation. That cannot happen in the case of the interference away from the ideal. In consequence, the expected interferences with the market generate a greater deviation from the competitive ideal than before even though the before case was not itself the competitive ideal. Of course, the closer the current quantity is to the ideal quantity, the greater the probability that the interference toward the ideal quantity will overshoot.

But even in the case where the interference toward the competitive ideal does not overshoot, we would expect the deadweight loss increased by an interference away from the competitive ideal to be greater than the deadweight loss reduced by a movement of the same magnitude toward that ideal. That statement holds for the kinds of supply and demand curves that economists expect.

Deadweight loss has two components. Let us measure it in the case of people receiving less of the product than the competitive optimum. One of the components is the foregone quantity. At each quantity foregone, the other component is the difference between the benefits people would have received and the cost of procuring that quantity. The benefit can be measured by the demand price for that quantity. The deadweight loss in this case is the sum (or integral) over the foregone quantity of the difference between the demand and supply prices. The foregone quantity is the difference between the competitive quantity and the actual quantity. An analogous measure is appropriate for the case of too much product produced, but in this case it is the positive difference between the supply price and the demand price that is relevant. In both of these cases deadweight loss is measured with respect to the competitive quantity determined if all the conditions of the competitive ideal were operative. The deadweight loss is measured in terms of the difference in the quantity actually produced and that competitive ideal.

For well-behaved demand and supply curves this deadweight loss increases more than proportionately with the magnitude of the difference between the true demand price and the true supply price. This greater than proportionality is produced because for standard supply and demand curves the difference between the quantity actually produced and the true competitive quantity is a positive function of the price difference. For example, for straight line demand and supply curves that quantity difference is proportional to the price difference.

Examine what that means for the expected deadweight loss when there is a market interference with an equal chance of moving away or closer to the competitive ideal quantity and there is no overshooting in the latter case. The increased deadweight loss from moving further away from the competitive ideal will be greater than the reduction in deadweight loss from moving closer to that ideal.

REFERENCES

Achen, Christopher and Larry Bartels, 2016, <u>Democracy for Realists: Why Elections Do Not Produce Responsive Government</u>, Princeton, Princeton University Press

Algan, Yann and Pierre Cahuc, 2010, "Inherited Trust and Growth", <u>American Economic Review</u>, 100, 2060-92

Althaus, Scott, 2001, <u>Collective Preferences in Democratic Politics</u>, Cambridge U.K., Cambridge University Press

Arnhart, Larry,1998, <u>Darwinian Natural Right,</u> Albany, State University of New York

Asch, S.E. 1963, "Effects of Group Pressure upon the Modification of Judgments," in <u>Groups, Leadership, and Men</u>, ed. Harold Guetzkow, New York. Russel and Russel

Ayer, A.J., <u>Language, Truth, and Logic</u>, 1936 London, Gollancz,

Bercussion, Brian, 2003,<u>European Labour Law and the Charter of Fundamental Rights</u>, The Transnational Trade Union Rights

Bergson, Abram, 1938 "A Reformulation of Certain Aspects of Welfare Economics," <u>Quarterly Journal of Economics</u>, 52(7), 314-44

Becker, Gary, 1983, "A Theory of Competition Among Pressure Groups for Political Influence," <u>Quarterly Journal of Economics</u>, 97, 371-400

Becker, G., K. Murphy, and I. Werning, 2005 "The Equilibrium Distribution of Income and the Market for Status", <u>The Journal of</u>

Political Economy, 113, 282-310

Berggren, N., H. Jordahl, and C. Stern, 2010"A Left-Right Divide: The Political Opinions of Swedish Social Scientists," Unpublished Manuscript, Stockholm, Ratio Institute

Blank, Rebecca, 2002, "Evaluating Welfare Reform in the United States", \NBER Working Paper No.8983

Blinder, Alan and Alan Krueger, 2004,"What Does the Public Know about Economic Policy and How Does it Know it?" Discussion Paper #1324, Bonn, Germany, IZA

Bonica, A., A. Chilton, and M. Mayo, 2015 "The Political Ideologies of American Lawyers", Journal of Legal Analysis forthcoming

Bonica, A., N. McCarty, K, Poole, and H. Rosenthal, 2013, "Why Hasn't Democracy Slowed Rising Inequality?" Journal of Economic Perspectives, 27 pp. 103-124

Boehm, Christopher, 1999, Hierarchy in the Forest, Cambridge, Mass, Harvard University Press

2012, Moral Origin s: The Evolution of Virtue, Altruism, and Shame, New York, Liberal Books,

Brooks, Arthur, New York Times, Dec. 20, 2013

Brooks, Clem,2014, "Nations, Classes, and the Politics of Professors" in Professors and Their Politics, ed by Neil Gross and Solon Simons, Baltimore, Johns Hopkins Press

Buchanan, James, 1980, The Economics and the Ethics of Constitutional Order, Ann Arbor, University of Michigan Press

Carlsson, Fredrik and Olaf Johansson-Stenman. 2010, Why Do You Vote and Vote the Way You Do. Kyklos 63, 495-516

Conard, Edward, 2013. Unintended Consequences: Why Everything You've Been Told About the Economy is Wrong, New York, Penguin, 2016. The Upside of Inequality: How Good Intentions Undermine sthe Middle Class, New York, Penguin

Congleton, Roger. 2007. The Moral Voter Hypothesis: Economic and Normative Aspects of Public Policy and Law within Democracies. Journal of Public Finance and Public Choice, 25, 3-30

D'Arge, R., Schulze, W., Brookshire, D. 1982, "Carbon Dioxide and Intergenerational Choice," American Economic Review, 72, 251-6

Diamond, Peter and Hausman, Jerry, 1993, "On Contingent Valuation Measurement of Nonuse Values," in Contingent Valuation: A Critical Assessment, ed. Jerry a Farber, Amsterdam, North Holland

Farber, Daniel, 1999 Eco-Pragmatism, Chicago, University of Chicago Press

Foster, Peter, 2014 Why We Bite the Invisible Hand: The Psychology of Anti Capitalism. Toronto, Pleasance Press

Fox News, Exit Poll Summary: Obama's Key Groups Made the Difference, Nov. 7. 2012

Frank, Robert, 1999 Luxury Fever: Why Money Fails to Satisfy in an Era of Excess, Princeton, Princeton University Press

Frey B., W. Pommerine, F. Schneider, Gilbert, G. 1984, Consensus and Dissension Among Economists: An Empirical Inquiry, *American Economic Review* American Economic Review, 74, 986-994

Friedman, Milton, 1953, Essays in Positive Economics. Chicago, The University of Chicago Press

Friedman, Milton and Rose, Free to Choose, 1990 New York, Harcourt

Froehlich, N., Oppenheimer, J., Eavey, C 1987., "Laboratory Results on Rawls's Distributive Justice," British Journal of Political Science, 17, 1-21

Fuchs, V., A. Krueger, and J. Poterba, 1998 "Economists' Views About Parameters, Values, and Policies" Journal of Economic Literature 36, 1387-1425

Fukuyama, Francis, 2011 The Origins of Political Order, Farrar, Straus, and Giroux

Gallup, George, "Presidential Preferences by Groups," Oct. 6, 2014

Gerber, Alan and Dean Karlan, 2006"Does the Media Matter? A Field Experiment Measuring Voting Behavior and Political Opinion, Yale Economic Applications an Policy, Discussion Paper #12

Gillens, Martin and Benjamin Page, 2014, "Testing Theories of American Politics", Perspectives on Politics. 12, 564-581

Greene, Kenneth and Phillip Nelson, 2007 "Is Relative Income of Overriding Importance for Individuals?" International Journal of Social Science, 34, 882-898,

Greene, Kenneth and Bong Yoon, 2004"Religiosity, Economics, and Life Satisfaction", Review of Social Economy, 62 245-261

Groseclose, Tim and Jeffrey Milyo, 2005, "A Measure of Media Bias," Quarterly Journal of Economics, 120, 1191-1237

Gross, Neil, 2013 Why Are Professors Liberal and Why Do Conservatives Care? Cambridge Ma., Harvard University Press

Gross, Neil and Simmons, Solon, 2007. "The Social and Political Views of American Professors," Working Paper, Harvard, Sept. 24

Haferkemp, A., D. Fetchenhaus, F. Belschak, and D. Enste , 2009 "Efficiency Versus Fairness: The Evaluation of Labor Market Policies by Economists and Laypeople".Journal of Economic Psychology, 30, 527-539

Haidt, Jonathan, 2012, The Righteous Mind: Why Good People Are Divided by Politics, New York, Pantheon, 2015, "The Yale Problem Begins in High School", Heterodox Academy

Hayek, Frederich, 1994, The Road to Serfdom, Chicago, The

University of Chicago Press, 1998, The Fatal Conceit: The Errors of Socialism, Chicago, The University of Chicago Press

Headey, Bruce, R. Muffet, and G. Wagner, 2007 "Long-running German Panel Survey Shows that Personal and Economic Choices, Just Not Genes Matter for Happiness", Proceedings of the National Academy of Sciences, 107, 17922-26

Highton, Benjamin ,2009, "Revisiting the Relationship between Educational Attainment and Political Sophistication, The Journal of Politics, 71, pp. 1564-1576

Holsey, Cheryl and Borcherding, Thomas, 1997, "Why Does Government's Share of National Income Grow? An Assessment of the Recent Literature on the U.S. Experience," in Perspectives on Public Choice: A Handbook, ed. Dennis Mueller, Cambridge, Cambridge University Press

Inglehart, R., Basan, ez, M., and Moreno, Al 1998, Human Values and Beliefs: A Cross-Cultural Source Book, Ann Arbor, The University of Michigan Press,

Jerit, Jennifer and Jason Barabas, (2009) "Partisan Perceptual Bias and the Information Environment", Journal of Politics, 74, pp. 672-684

Jost, John, Glaser, Jack, Kruglanksi, Aria, and Sulloway, Frank, 2003, "Political Conservatism as Motivated Social Cognition", Psychological Bulletin 129

Kasperowitz, Peter and Russel Berman, 2011, "Balanced Budget Amendment Comes Up Short in the House," The Hill, November 11

Kazemipur, A., 2006, " Canadian Exceptionalism? Trust and Diversity in Canadian Cities" Journal of International Migration and Integration", 7, 219-40

Kimball, Roger, 2008 Tenured Radicals: How Politics Has Corrupted Our Higher Education, Third Edition Chicago, Ivan R. Dee

Klein, Daniel and C. Stern, 2007 "Is there a Free-Market Economist in the House? "The Policy Views of American Economic Association Members", The American Journal of Economics and Sociology, 66, pp. 309-334

Kuklinski, J., P. Quirk, J. Jerit, D. Schweider, and R. Rich,(2000)," Misinformation and the Currency of Democratic Citizenship", Journal of Politics, 62, 790-816

Laband, David and Hussain, Anwar, 2005 "The Tragedy of the Political Commons: Evidence from U.S. Senate Roll Call Votes on Environmental Legislation,",Public Choice, 124 353-64,

MaCurdy, Thomas, "How Effective is the Minimum Wage at Supporting the Poor", Thomas, 2015 Journal of Political Economy, 123 pp. 497-545

Mar, R., K. Oatley, and J. Peterson, 2009, "Exploring the Link Between Reading Fiction and Empathy: Ruling Out Individual Differences and Examining Outcomes," Communications, 34, pp.407-428

Marwick, Arthur,2000 The Sixties: Cultural Revolution in Britain, France, Italy and the United States

Merline, John, 2014, Investor Business Daily, 02/27

Mincer, J. and S. Polachek, 1974 "Family Investments in Human Capital: Earnings of Women," Journal of Political Economics, 82 part II 76-100

Milgrom, Paul, 1993 "Is Sympathy an Economic Value?" in Contingent Valuation: A Critical Assessment, ed. Jerry Hausman, New York, Elsevier

Miller, David, 1992 "Distributive Justice: What the People Think," Ethics, 102, pp. 555-592

Mulligan, Casey 2013, The Redistribution Recession: How Labor Market Distortions Contracted the Economy, New York, Oxford University Press, The Celebration of the Life and Work of Gary Becker, 2014

National Council of State Legislatures, 1999 "State Balance Budget Requirements", April 12

Nakhaie, Reza and Robert Brym, 1999 "The Political Attitudes of Canadian Professors", Canadian Journal of Sociology, 24, 329-53

National Education Association, 2014 "2013-14 NEA Resolutions

National Opinion Research Center ORC) 1996, General Social Surveys, 1972-1996, Ann Arbor: Inter-university Consortium for Political and Social Research

Nelson, Phillip and Greene, Kenneth, 2003 Signaling Goodness: Social Rules and Public Choice, Ann Arbor, University of Michigan Press

Neumark, David and William Washer, 2006 Minimum Wages and Employment: A Review of Evidence from the New Minimum Wage Research, National Bureau of Economic Research Working Paper No. 12663

Nordhaus, William and Boyer, Joseph, 2000 Warming the World: Economic Models of Global Warming, Cambridge Mass., MIT Press 1973

Nozick, Rober 1974t, Anarchy, State, and Utopia, New York, Liberal Books

Peterson, Paul, 2014 How the Education Spendthrifts Get Away With It, Wall Street Journal, September 22

Ofek, Haim, 2001 Second Nature: Economic Origins of Human Evolution, Cambridge, Cambridge University Press

Page, Benjamin and Robert Shapiro, 1992, The Rational Public: Fifty Years of Trends in Americans' Policy Preferences, Chicago, The University of Chicago Press

Peltzman, Sam, 1980 "The Growth of Government," Journal of Law and Economics, 23, 209-97

Pinker, Steven, 2002 The Blank Slate, New York, Penguin

O'Neil, Tyler, 2017, PJ Media, Jan.

Rawls, J.A 1990 "Utilitarian Ethics and Democratic Government", Ethics, 335-348

Sapolsky, Robert, 2014 "Mind and Matter", Wall Street Journal, July 9

Sen, Amartya, 2001 "Democracy as a Universal Value" in The Global Divergence of Democracy, Diamond, Larry and Plattner, Marc eds. John Hopkins University Press

Silberman, Laurence, 1990-91 "The ABA and Judicial Nominations," George Washington Law Review, 1092

Singer, Peter, 1981 The Expanding Circle: Ethics and Sociobiology, Straus and Giroux, New York

Sowell, Thomas 2002, A Conflict of Vision, New York, Liberal Books

Stern, Nicholas, 2006 Review on the Economics of Climate Change, London, His Majesty's Treasury

Schuessler, Alexander, 2000, A Logic of Expressive Choice, Princeton, Princeton

Somin, Ilya, 2013, Democracy and Political Ignorance: Why Smaller Government is Smarter, Palo Alto, Stanford University Press

Stiglitz, Joseph, 2012 The Price of Inequality. How Today's Divided Society Endangers Our Future, Norton

Stigler, George, 1971 "The Theory of Economic Regulation," Bell Journal of Economics and Management Science, 2 3-21

Stiglitz, Joseph, 2015, The Great Divide: Unequal Societies and What We Can Do About Them, Norton, New York

Sunstein, Cass, 2014"Talking Like Grown Ups about Climate Change" Bloomberg Views The Week, May 6,

Volkh, Eugene, 2015"The Volkh Conspiracy", The Washington Post,Jun

Walzer, Michael 1983 Spheres of Justice: A Defense of Pluralism and Equality, New York, Liberal Books

Weeden, Jason and Robert Kurzhan, 2014 The Hidden Agenda of the Political Mind: How Self Interest Shapes Our Opinions and Why We Won't Admit It, Princeton, Princeton University Press

Wilson, David Sloan, 2015 Does Altruism Exist? Culture,Genes, and the Welfare of Others, New Haven, Yale University Press

Wilson, E.O., 1992, The Diversity of Life, Cambridge, Harvard University Press

Wood, Peter and Tascano, Michael, 2013, What Does Bowdoin Teach: How a Contemporary Liberal Arts College Shapes Students, New York, National Association of Scholars

Yezer, A., Goldfarb, R and Poppen .P, 1996 " Does Studying Economics Discourage Cooperation: Watch What We Do Not What We Say or Play," The Journal of Economic Perspectives, 10, 177-86

Zak, Paul, 2011, "The Physiology of Moral Sentiment" Journal of Economic Behavior and Organization, 77, 53-66

ENDNOTES

¹

2   Brooks (2014) looks at professorial attitudes relative to country attitudes for a variety of issues. Only one of those issues is directly about the economy:: are you in favor of the welfare state. He finds that professors in most countries are opposed to the welfare state relative to others in the country, and this goes for the United States as well. But we have substantial evidence that professors are more liberal on economic issues in the United States, so his results are an anomaly and, hence, questionable. Somehow the question is invoking confused responses. But whatever the reason for this crazy result, the professorate in the United States has attitudes on this question right in the middle of the pack of professors' attitudes from other countries, so is some slight confirmation that the attitude of professors in the United States is at least in part an international phenomenon. One other question about gender equality has economic overtones. For that question the United States and nearly all other countries have the expected liberal professorate.

CPSIA information can be obtained
at www.ICGtesting.com
Printed in the USA
LVHW091400211220
674768LV00029B/167